Praise for Sue Tabashnik's first book, *The Fans' Love Story: How the Movie* 'DIRTY DANCING' *Captured the Hearts of Millions!*

"Your book is both great journalism and original writing. It is a very positive testament to Patrick and his life as an Artist and the impact it had on others."

—Joshua Sinclair. Director, writer, producer of Jump! *and multiple other films and television shows; physician, professor. Austria*

"Patrick Swayze captured the hearts of millions with dirty dancing twenty years ago. *The Fans' Love Story: How the Movie* 'DIRTY DANCING' *Captured the Hearts of Millions!* explores the fans' fascination with the work and how it made them life-long fans of Swayze and the film. As Sue Tabashnik interviews fans to get an idea of why the film gained so much popularity, and much more, *The Fans' Love Story* is of strong interest to any fan of the film, highly recommended."

—Midwest Book Review

"Wow! Sue, you did an amazing thing! You should be so very proud of your work and of the gift you gave to all of us who participated in your labor of love. Thank you from the bottom of my heart for introducing me to so many people who share my depth of connection to Baby, Johnny, and the entire *Dirty Dancing* experience."

—Debbie Wallerstein. Deerfield Beach, Florida

"Every *Dirty Dancing* or Patrick Swayze fan will want this book. It is filled with insights on the movie and Patrick from many different perspectives. Personal accounts from people behind the scenes along with photos of the movie location give the reader a sense of being there. Fans' comments and personal observations from people who were there during production help to round out this wonderful reading experience and brings fans a little closer to knowing Patrick as a person."

—*Ingrid Mennella. Inverness, Florida*

"This book is a must-have for any Patrick Swayze and/or *Dirty Dancing* fan! The interviews with the people involved with the film are fantastic and give you a rare glimpse into the world of *Dirty Dancing* and the Catskills. The book also reminds us all of that magical moment when we found our first love. Feel the magic of the movie again and see how it touched and continues to touch lives all over the world."

—*Jan Griffith. Elgin, Texas*

"Wonderful, well written, interesting, and fun to read. So many extras, very informative. A must for every Patrick Swayze and *Dirty Dancing* fan. Highly recommended."

—*Rosemarie Ravenelle. Putnam, Connecticut*

"I have to admit that at first I was a bit skeptical, thinking, *What is left to write in addition to all that has already been said before about this wonderful movie?* But this book is such an excellent must-have addition for every true *Dirty Dancing*/Patrick Swayze fan! It conveys so much extra info and insights of people who were close to the filming of this movie in one way or another, as well as thoughts and emotions of so many different people from all over the world. I am sure the next time I will be watching *Dirty Dancing*, I will view it with different eyes, having in mind so many new perspectives! Great job, Sue—thank you very much for this detailed overview on one of my favorite films!"

—*Baerbel von Scheven. Germany*

DEAR DIRTY DANCING FAN,
LET'S "DIRTY-DANCE" THROUGH
LIFE & "SPREAD THE LOVE!"
BEST WISHES,
SUE TABASHNIK

The Fans' Love Story
ENCORE

5/3/17

Dear Jeanie,
I do hope you enjoyed reading about my film "Dirty Dancing" - I had x - was very honest, true & real to write. May you have many happy days - they really were the best of times -
Fondly Jackie Horner

A portion of the proceeds from the sale of this book will be donated to the Patrick Swayze Pancreas Cancer Research Fund at the Stanford Cancer Institute.

ALSO BY SUE TABASHNIK

The Fans' Love Story:
How the Movie 'DIRTY DANCING' *Captured the Hearts of Millions!*

The Fans' Love Story

ENCORE

Sue Tabashnik

Walled Lake, Michigan

The Fans' Love Story Encore:
How the Movie DIRTY DANCING *Captured the Hearts of Millions!*

© 2013 by Sue Tabashnik. All rights reserved.

www.likedirtydancing.com

Cover images © 2013 by Patricia Bacall, Bacall: Creative. All rights reserved.

This book is an independent publication and is not associated with or authorized by Lionsgate or any other person/entity associated with the movie *Dirty Dancing*. All references in this book to the movie are for the purpose of commentary, analysis, and literary discussion only.

Furthermore, this book is not associated with or authorized or approved by Lisa Niemi Swayze or the Patrick Swayze Pancreas Cancer Research Fund at the Stanford Cancer Institute. The decision to donate a portion of the proceeds from the sale of this book to the above fund is strictly the author's idea and wish.

The views and opinions expressed by the interviewees and other third-party sources in this book are not necessarily those of the author, and the author accepts no responsibility for inaccuracies or omissions by interviewees or other third party sources.

This book may not be reproduced, transmitted, or stored in whole or in part by any means, including graphic, electronic, or mechanical, without the express written consent of the author except in the case of brief quotations embodied in critical articles and reviews.

ISBN 978-0-9894086-0-8 (pbk)
ISBN 978-0-9894086-1-5 (ebook)

PRINTED IN THE UNITED STATES OF AMERICA

Book and cover design: Patricia Bacall

COPYRIGHT PERMISSIONS

I gratefully thank these sources for giving permission to use their material.

ACKNOWLEDGMENT OF GRATITUDE

1. From *PATRICK SWAYZE* © 1988 by Mitchell Krugel. Reprinted by permission of St. Martin's Press. All rights reserved.

CHAPTER ONE

1. © 2008 by Broadwayfanclub.com. "Dirty Dancing: A Legendary Story on National Tour." The Broadway League. August 2008 Newsletter.
2. © 2009 by *Jewish Journal of Greater Los Angeles*. "'Dirty Dancing' Comes Alive on Stage." Rick Schultz. May 20, 2009.
3. © 2008 by *Chicago Tribune*. "'Dirty Dancing' creator keeps the legend alive." Sid Smith. September 28, 2008.

4. © 2005 by *Globe Newspaper Company*. "Stayin' Alive." Mark Shanahan. *The Boston Globe*. September 29, 2005.
5. © 1988 by ABC. *Barbara Walters Special Interview*. ABC News. May 11, 1988.
6. © 2006 by Whatsonstage.com. "Photos: Swayze & Sweeney Ready to Play in Dolls." Terri Paddock. June 5, 2006.
7. © 2008 by FemaleFirst.co.uk. "Miranda Garrison talks Dirty Dancing." September 2, 2008.
8. © 2006 by Guardian News & Media. "Patrick Swayze on 'Dirty Dancing.'" Telegraph.co.uk. September 23, 2006.

CHAPTER TWO

1. © 2012 by *East Anglian Daily Times*. "Still having the time of our lives at Dirty Dancing." David Henshall. August 24, 2012.
2. © 2012 by ABCnews.com. Diane Sawyer. "Jennifer Grey Reveals 'Dirty Dancing' Secrets." ABC News. August 24, 2012.
3. © 2010 by Jezebel.com. "*Dirty Dancing* Is The Greatest Movie Of All Time." Irin Carmon. April 29, 2010.
4. © 2011 by Popdose.com. "The Popdose Interview: Franke Previte." Rob Smith. August 8, 2011.
5. From *PATRICK SWAYZE* © 1988 by Mitchell Krugel. Reprinted by permission of St. Martin's Press. All rights reserved.

CHAPTER FOUR

1. © 2011 by *Daily Mail*. "Patrick Swayze's widow Lisa Niemi recreates Dirty Dancing scene as she unveils waxwork model at Madame Tussauds." Mike Larkin. October 19, 2011.

CHAPTER SIX

1. © by Maurice Williams. "Maurice Williams & the Zodiacs Discography."

CHAPTER SEVEN

1. © by Jackie Horner. "Biographical Sketch—Jackie Horner."

CHAPTER FIFTEEN

1. From *PATRICK SWAYZE* © 1988 by Mitchell Krugel. Reprinted by permission of St. Martin's Press. All rights reserved.
2. © 2010 by Jezebel.com. "*Dirty Dancing* Is The Greatest Movie Of All Time." Irin Carmon. April 29, 2010.
3. © 2011 by *Hollywood Reporter*. "Kenny Ortega to Direct 'Dirty Dancing' Remake." Jay A. Fernandez. August 8, 2011.

CLOSING

1. © 2012 by ITV.com. "'Dirty Dancing' celebrates its 25th anniversary." ITV News. August 22, 2012.

To my Mom,
Phyllis Friedman,

To my Dad,
David Tabashnik,

who believed in me and gave to me
the precious gift of unconditional love.

I love you, Mom and Dad,
and will always have you in my heart.
I strive to follow what you taught me—
to be kind to others, to value family, to do
what is right, and to treat life as precious.

ACKNOWLEDGMENT OF GRATITUDE

To Mr. Patrick Swayze,

who is still inspiring—helping me through challenging times and motivating me to follow my dreams.

I am so grateful to have met you, to have your wonderful legacy of work to enjoy, and to have your *amazing spirit*—whose light shines so bright—as such an inspiration.

> **"Very early I learned that you have to be true to yourself about what you care about—what you believe in. If you're not, you have nothing at all. You have to listen to that little bird inside that tells you what's right."**
>
> —Patrick Swayze[1]

CONTENTS

INTRODUCTION

Why write another book on *Dirty Dancing*? With the amazing milestone of *Dirty Dancing* turning twenty-five years old in August 2012 and people still just not getting enough of the movie, it seemed like there was more to tell about *Dirty Dancing*. And I discovered that I was right.

In this book, I strived to put out new information regarding *Dirty Dancing* and to continue to capture the magic of this iconic film with many stories and photos.

I was extremely fortunate to be granted an amazing, very detailed interview with Linda Gottlieb, producer of *Dirty Dancing*, about what really happened regarding getting *Dirty Dancing* filmed. The songwriter and performer Maurice Williams (of Maurice Williams & the Zodiacs), whose song "Stay" is in the movie, provided a wonderful, warm interview regarding his famous song and his special take on the movie, and his photo and discography. Jackie Horner, story consultant to *Dirty Dancing* and dance pro in the Catskills, divulged more behind-the-scenes information (with numerous fantastic anecdotes about the real Catskills goings-on that were used in the movie), provided photos of the Catskills, and shared her special journey with *Dirty Dancing*.

I was very lucky to interview Jim and Karen Myers—head chef and dining room manager, respectively, at Mountain Lake Hotel in Virginia during the filming of *Dirty Dancing*. They had many interesting and amusing stories to tell; including their experiences with some of the stars.

I also was very fortunate to have the opportunity to interview Tom and Patt Rocks, who were dance extras during the filming of *Dirty Dancing* in Lake Lure, North Carolina; they shared their interactions with the stars and how being in the movie touched their lives. The Rocks referred me to Betty Rollins (Patt's sister), who was also a dance extra on the same set, for another appealing interview. Mrs. Rollins actually was so interested in my journey of writing my first book and now this second book on *Dirty Dancing* that the last part of my discussion with her became more of an interview of me, for which I am grateful. The candid photos from the set provided by Mrs. Rollins and the Rocks are just wonderful and are such a great addition to the book.

And how can I not touch on the fact that Patrick Swayze, who did such an iconic portrayal of the character Johnny Castle in *Dirty Dancing* and co-wrote and sang "She's Like the Wind," is sorely missed by so many people. Joshua Sinclair, who wrote, produced, and directed one of Patrick Swayze's last movies, *Jump!*, shares a wonderful, heart-felt tribute to his friend and colleague. Thank you to Mr. Sinclair for graciously allowing me to include his tribute and the poster of *Jump!* in the book.

Speaking of tributes to Patrick Swayze, the staff of Madame Tussauds Hollywood shared an informative, warm interview about the 2011 Patrick Swayze *Dirty Dancing* statue, along with two fabulous photos. All of this was made possible by Rowena Adalid, head of marketing, to whom I am grateful. In December 2012, I was very lucky to have the opportunity to travel to Madame Tussauds Hollywood and see this wonderful, much-deserved tribute. It really was such an intense, sentimental, bittersweet experience; but I would not trade it for the world. The timing of my trip there was really important to me and gave me a precious lift that helped me deal with a tough time in my life.

Of course, without the fans, the movie would not be the cultural phenomenon that it is. This book includes heartfelt and deeply personal tributes from fans of varying ages and from three continents; who each share the special impact that *Dirty Dancing* has had on them, for which I am grateful.

Finally, I have re-published chapter one from my first book, which discusses my connection to *Dirty Dancing*, the history of the film and the many forms it has taken, and why the movie continues to be so popular. I have an update on the above-mentioned topics which includes a multitude of key happenings that have occurred since 2010, such as the twenty-fifth anniversary of the movie, the continuing success of the stage show, Jennifer Grey's participation on the 2010 season of *Dancing with the Stars*, the continuing popularity of the smash-hit "(I've Had) The Time of My Life," a controversial remake in the works, and the impact of Patrick Swayze's portrayal of Johnny Castle on the success of the movie and on so many people.

So, *Dirty Dancing* fans new and old, sit back, relax, reminisce, and enjoy another *Dirty Dancing* trip to celebrate this amazing, heart-warming, iconic film.

CHAPTER ONE

MY CONNECTION TO *DIRTY DANCING* AND WHY I THINK IT CONTINUES TO GO ON AND ON

This chapter originally appeared as chapter one in my first book, *The Fans' Love Story: How the Movie 'DIRTY DANCING' Captured the Hearts of Millions!*

"That was the summer of 1987," and I followed my usual weekend passion of going to a movie. Little did I know how much watching this particular movie would change my life. The movie happened to be *Dirty Dancing*. Need I say more? I confess that I was one of "those women" who saw the movie multiple times. Yes, I became a member of the "100 club." At that "time of my life," I had recently gone through a very difficult break-up with the man that I thought was my soul mate. Watching this movie not only provided a very nice escape, but also seemed to impart that all again would be right in the world—that true love could exist against tremendous odds. I came to the conclusion that watching this movie was very soothing, even better than reading self-help books, and in a way just as good as counseling. The story was great, the music was fantastic, and the dancing was powerful. Finally, there was this sizzling, passionate actor/dancer by the name of Mr. Patrick Swayze, who played the lead heartthrob (the "Nobody puts Baby in a corner" guy). I was hooked into becoming a huge fan of Mr. Swayze. The more I watched his work, heard him give interviews, and read about him, the bigger my connection became to him.

After one contact with a fan club in 1987 (I received an autographed picture of Mr. Swayze), the years went by with me still being an avid fan. While searching the Internet in 2000, I struck gold, and found an active fan club—The Official Patrick Swayze International Fan Club, and big surprise, I joined! I really didn't have any idea what to expect. Was I living out some adolescent fantasy by joining? What the heck! The dues were reasonable, and I would be receiving quarterly magazines and pictures—and hopefully could learn more about Mr. Swayze. After all, I didn't have to tell anybody that I was a member. I had never contemplated contacting a Hollywood star before, and I had certainly never pictured myself belonging to a fan club. Was I now a groupie? I had a picture in my mind of Elvis fans swooning at Graceland and of hysterical women following stars around the country. After mailing in my dues, I had an immediate response from the club president, Mrs. Margaret Howden from Scotland, and felt welcomed into this group. Soon, I could see that this was serious business, and that there were others who had "this thing" for Mr. Swayze. Maybe I wasn't losing my marbles after all.

Actually, as it has turned out, I have enjoyed many different activities through the fan club. I met Mr. Swayze four times—and had the opportunity to hold conversations with him individually and as part of a group. I met him at two dance benefits for the extraordinary dance company Complexions Contemporary Ballet—right here in Detroit—in 2002 and then again in 2004. I also met Mr. Swayze and Ms. Niemi at two film festivals—WorldFest-Houston International Film Festival in 2003 and Nashville Film Festival in 2004—that were showing their magnificent dance movie, *One Last Dance*. Their accessibility to us fans at both of the film festivals was really amazing. Then, in 2005, I had the opportunity to call in a question to Mr. Swayze on *The Big Idea with Donny Deutsch* CNBC television show.

Throughout the years, I have had the good fortune to make some long-lasting, great friendships with some of the other fans in the club. I have also been able to develop my writing skills and use my creativity by writing twelve articles that were published in the fan club magazine. Finally, it has been very special and wonderful to be part of a community supporting someone who was not only enormously talented as an actor, dancer, singer, song writer, producer, and choreographer, but who was also about traditional values, family, a solid work ethic, integrity, spirituality, passion, and activities (such as advocating for the arts, conservation, and cancer research) to make the world a better place. And I need to mention how Mr. Swayze loved animals, especially Arabian horses, and his support to The Arabian Horse Association.

As mentioned in the Introduction, I started writing this book in 2007, long before Mr. Swayze was diagnosed with cancer. It was absolutely heartbreaking and devastating to find out about Mr. Swayze's Stage IV pancreatic cancer diagnosis. As part of the community supporting him prior to the cancer diagnosis and after the diagnosis, I have always considered it to be a privilege. I was and will continue to be amazed and inspired by him—by his wonderful spirit and heroic battle for life.

I have read Mr. Swayze's guestbook since becoming a fan club member in 2000, and read it more closely and more often following Mr. Swayze's cancer diagnosis. I can tell you that there are thousands and thousands of messages that were sent to him from fans of all ages (five and up) and from all over the world, telling how much they love *Dirty Dancing* and what a special part *Dirty Dancing* has played and will continue to play in their lives.

In addition, *Dirty Dancing* has scored very high in numerous polls and surveys. In February 2008, the *Daily Mail* in the United Kingdom reported that *Dirty Dancing* has the number one most romantic quote ever: Baby saying, "I'm scared of walking out of this room and never feeling for the rest of my whole life the way I feel when I am with you." Also, the *Daily Mail* printed a story on May 6, 2007 that listed *Dirty Dancing* as the number-one movie that women watch. In July 2005, the *Scotsman* ran a story that reported the water lift scene was voted number one as the most favorite scene of all time in a poll answered by almost 1,200 people. In February 2008, per ananova.com an online DVD rental delivery service, LOVEFILM.com listed *Dirty Dancing* as the second best "feel-good" movie. Per an E! Entertainment Television 2007 poll of industry executives and celebrities, *Dirty Dancing* was named as one of the Top Ten Date movies of all time. According to ITV in 2004, around 200,000 people in the United Kingdom voted *Dirty Dancing* as their favorite of 100 movies. In May 2009, *Dirty Dancing* won as Britain's favorite film in an online poll conducted by the Cinema Advertising Association. Finally, there are three other fun examples of the continuing popularity of *Dirty Dancing* that I just cannot leave out. In a February 21, 2008 survey done by UK Cinema Industry for the "best movie couple," Ms. Grey and Mr. Swayze came in third place. Among female voters, *Dirty Dancing* took second place (lost to *Ghost*) in the best screen kiss poll conducted in the UK by Denplan in honor of the 13th annual National Kissing Day in July 2008. In a 2009 Valentine's Day poll done by HMV, *Ghost* was number one for the best love film, and *Dirty Dancing* placed second.

The stage version of *Dirty Dancing*, written by Ms. Eleanor Bergstein, the writer/co-producer of the movie, has been a brilliant success in Australia (the world premiere was in Sydney in 2004), New Zealand, Germany, and London's West End. In November 2007, the stage show opened in Toronto—with 1.65 million in first-day ticket sales. Next, the production opened in the Netherlands and then in the United States—first stop was Chicago (September 28, 2008), then Boston (February 8, 2009), and finally Los Angeles (April 28, 2009). There is speculation that the next US stop will be Broadway, and by the time that you are reading this book, maybe that will have occurred.

Multiple sources indicate that for about seventeen years, Ms. Bergstein resisted doing the stage play, but then realized that the audience wanted to be there—to be more intensely involved in the experience—and thus she determined that this would be satisfied by a theatrical experience. In an interview "Dirty Dancing: A Legendary Story on National Tour" that Ms. Bergstein gave to The Broadway Fan Club in August 2008, Ms. Bergstein was asked, "What was your starting point when you set out to reconceive this hit movie as a stage production?" Ms. Bergstein answered, "I wanted to find a way to transform it into a new kind of theatrical event . . . I wanted a form that would honor our open-hearted audience . . . And one that might bring into the theatre a new audience that has had its most profound experiences at movies and rock concerts."[1] Rick Schultz in *The Jewish Journal* "'Dirty Dancing' Comes Alive on Stage" on May 20, 2009 wrote, "Bergstein said she waited until 2004 to do a stage adaptation because 'it seemed that the film stood by itself, and I never wanted the audience to feel I was taking advantage of them just to make money.'"[2] Furthermore, Mr. Schultz reported, ". . . despite being two decades old, the movie's continuing popularity suggested to Bergstein that 'people might want to step through the flat screen and have it happen around them, and that meant live theater.'"[2] Finally, Mr. Schultz wrote that Ms. Bergstein said, "Everybody has a secret dancer inside them . . . It's dancing that makes you feel, 'That could be me.'"[2] To sum up, Eleanor Bergstein was asked in The Broadway Fan Club interview— Q: "What has made this story appeal to audiences for so long?" EB: "I think it's that everyone has a secret dancer inside them that they dream will connect them to the physical world in the way they desire. It is in all of us waiting to be tapped."[1] A final note is that the hopeful, change-oriented political climate of the '60s is focused on more in the stage version than in the movie.

Several sources report that Mr. Josef Brown from Australia, who has been playing Johnny in the current stage show all over the world since 2004, has stated that the *Dirty Dancing* movie influenced him to pursue and to commit to a dance career. Per Sid Smith in the *Chicago Tribune*, September 28, 2008, Josef Brown said, "For kids like me, in a tough, all-boys school, the movie told of this guy who was a street kid and yet vulnerable too. It's OK to be masculine. But it's OK to dance as well."[3] There have been many other comments in the media as to how Mr. Swayze's portrayal of the character Johnny has encouraged and inspired men to dance.

On May 1 and 2, 2007, to celebrate the 20th anniversary of *Dirty Dancing*, there were showings of the Lionsgate new digital re-mastered 35mm print of *Dirty Dancing* with a twenty-minute clip about *Dirty Dancing* in about 330 theaters across the US, and 45 in Canada. Of course I attended, and was really struck by the varied age group of the audience and how everyone was really getting into the movie—myself included. From August 24–30, 2007, *Dirty Dancing* was shown at The Ziegfeld in New York (with a special Q & A with Kelly Bishop) to once again celebrate the twenty-year mark. In September and October 2007, a new show, *The Music of Dirty Dancing*, toured around the United Kingdom. On November 6, 2007, Mr. Swayze made a wonderful, surprise appearance on *The Oprah Winfrey Show* to dance with Julia Boggio from the YouTube couple, Julia Boggio and James Derbyshire (from the United Kingdom). This couple's wedding video—which shows them doing the *Dirty Dancing* finale dance—had at that point been seen by more than two million YouTube viewers. At the end of 2007, *Dirty Dancing—The Video Game* was released by Codemasters.

Regarding other recent and/or ongoing *Dirty Dancing* activity, people from all over the world visit the locations where *Dirty Dancing* was filmed—Mountain Lake Hotel (Virginia) and Lake Lure Inn (North Carolina)—on a regular basis. (See separate sections on each location.) Mountain Lake Hotel has had *Dirty Dancing* weekends for years. In August 2007, Mountain Lake Hotel was the host of a United Kingdom television show—*Dirty Dancing: The Time of your Life Reality Series-Season 1* in which ten one-hour episodes were filmed in thirty days. In June 2008, the filming of the second season of the show occurred. Ms. Miranda Garrison, the assistant choreographer and Vivian in the movie, was one of the judges for the shows. One of the most popular activities for guests at Mountain Lake throughout the years has been to have their picture taken with a life-size cutout picture of Patrick Swayze per Mr. H. M. "Buzz" Scanland, Jr., General Manager at Mountain Lake Hotel. In October 2007, *Seriously Dirty Dancing* (parts filmed at both Mountain Lake Hotel and Lake Lure Inn) a British documentary narrated by Dawn Porter (who reportedly saw the movie around 200 times) was aired.

In November 2008, *Dirty Dancing: The Ultimate Girls' Night In Collector's Pack* (DVD of movie, commentary, outtakes, and a night dress, washbag, eye mask, etc.) was released by Lionsgate. Also, in December 2008, the Lionsgate DVD, "*Dirty Dancing:* Official Dance Workout" became available. In March 2009, BBC aired *Let's Dance for Comic Relief* created by Whizz Kid Entertainment (United Kingdom). The show had contestants re-enact famous dances, which included a performance by Paddy McGuiness and Keith Lemon to "(I've Had) The Time of My Life" from *Dirty Dancing*. Money received from callers who voted for their favorite routines was given to Comic Relief. On August 19, 2009, multiple sources reported that per *Production Weekly*, Lionsgate is doing a remake of the movie. Only time will tell if this is indeed true. I think that you will find it interesting to read what the fans in this book say about a *Dirty Dancing* sequel—which may give some insight as to how popular a remake would be.

Thus, *Dirty Dancing* continues to go on and on. I can't resist commenting that this independent movie was made on a shoe-string budget with virtually no violence (Johnny does briefly fight Robbie in one scene), no special effects, no weirdness, and yet it has remained popular for over twenty years.

What makes *Dirty Dancing* such a phenomenon? For me, I know that all I have to do to get a quick shot of "feel-good" is throw the

DVD in, sit back, and be captured by the bliss of *Dirty Dancing*. Whether I have been in a great mood and wanted a "fix," or whether I have been in a funk (like when my mother was lying in ICU, possibly going to die, about five years ago), I just had to pop in *Dirty Dancing* and could escape into a great place where there was love, integrity, and a happy ending. (I am not saying that seeing *Dirty Dancing* took away all of my stress regarding my mother's illness, but it did serve as an anchor to hope for me.) Furthermore, watching *Dirty Dancing* is kind of like meeting up with an old friend. Mr. Swayze spoke to *The Boston Globe's* Mark Shanahan in September 2005 about his and his wife's prized dance movie, *One Last Dance* (which they had just been to Slovakia to promote), and what he said can be applied to *Dirty Dancing* as well: "Everywhere we take this film, people want something to make them feel good. Hope is a big thing." He was also asked why audiences respond so strongly to dance. He said, "The world loves dance. It's our first form of worship. It's primal. Moving to rhythm is a powerful thing that's innate in all of us."[4] Mr. Swayze has made statements throughout the years that a big component of dancing with a partner is having a soul connection through the eyes. In his portrayal of Johnny and Ms. Grey's portrayal of Baby, the connection definitely happens, which is highlighted in one of the movie's songs, "Hungry Eyes" (written by Franke Previte and John DeNicola, and performed by Eric Carmen). By the way, the soundtrack to the movie has sold more than 42 million copies.

To think that Mr. Swayze almost didn't do *Dirty Dancing*! During the *ABC Barbara Walters Special Interview* in 1988, Mr. Swayze stated that he had been advised not to do the movie. However, he took the role because, "I felt something for Johnny, the guy from the streets . . . that is fighting to like himself, to believe in himself." It seems that Mr. Swayze put his own constant quest for personal/spiritual growth into the character of Johnny. He shared with Barbara Walters that he had backed off accepting "teenage idol" movie roles after *Skatetown USA* so that he could become a more accomplished actor. He said, "I was willing to bank on that with enough study and growth, and enough connection with myself and the truth in me, that I could become an actor to be reckoned with." Barbara Walters asked why do so many women watch the movie so many times. In response, he spoke about how the relationship between the two main characters was based on what is inside: "Everybody dreams that somebody would see into their lonely world . . . that would see past the exterior and see what they're really like . . . somebody sees through that and cares about them as a person . . . a relationship not because of how somebody swings their rear but because of what's inside . . ."[5]

Mr. Swayze has indicated throughout the years that key to *Dirty Dancing* is how Johnny and Baby connect with their hearts and souls, which is reflected in the movie's smash hit, "She's Like the Wind" (written by Mr. Swayze and Mr. Widelitz, and performed by Mr. Swayze, featuring Wendy Fraser). The song was #3 on *Billboard* Hot 100 and #1 on Adult Contemporary. In 1989, "She's Like the Wind" won at the BMI Film & TV Awards for "most performed song from a film." In April 2009, BMI (Broadcast Music, Inc.) reported that "She's Like the Wind" had officially charted its four millionth public performance. It is widely thought that Mr. Swayze was inspired by his wife in the writing of this hit song.

Per a June 5, 2006 Whatsonstage.com interview conducted by Terri Paddock in London, England—"Photos: Swayze & Sweeney Ready to Play in Dolls"—Mr. Swayze talked about the continuing popularity of the movie *Dirty Dancing*. "He (Mr. Swayze) attributes the success of 'the movie that wouldn't die' to the passion, and lack of ego, behind the original project . . . Mr. Swayze's words: 'When something works, it's really about heart.'"[6] Key *Dirty Dancing* people have indicated that Mr. Emile Ardolino's role as director was an important reason why *Dirty Dancing* worked so well—including his story-telling ability—especially by using dancing and humanness to make a film that touches the heart. Mr. Swayze has indicated in multiple media sources that Jennifer's Grey portrayal of Baby was totally amazing and really paramount to the movie.

Many of the principal people involved in creating/acting in *Dirty Dancing* have made statements to various media sources that they really enjoyed and appreciated the collaborative experience of making this movie. In a September 2, 2008 interview by FemaleFirst.co.uk, "Miranda Garrison talks Dirty Dancing," Ms. Garrison was asked if she had fond memories of making *Dirty Dancing*. She replied, "My memories of making this film are fantastic. I honestly 'had the time of my life!' . . . We original 'Dirty Dance People' contributed so much of our personal life stories to this film. This 'collective' storytelling has become an enormous validation of our youth and artistic philosophy."[7] Of course, "(I've Had) The Time of My Life" (written by Frank Previte, Donald Markowitz, and John DeNicola and performed by Bill Medley and Jennifer Warnes) won an Oscar, a Grammy, and a Golden Globe in 1988.

Referencing the above-mentioned interview of Miranda Garrison, while responding to the question—did she know that the lift scene she choreographed would become such an iconic scene, Ms. Garrison's words give us additional insight into the collaborative nature of the filmmakers and why the movie is so successful. Ms. Garrison answered, "To set the record straight, Kenny Ortega, myself and likely Patrick Swayze presented many 'lifts' to the director Emile Ardolino and writer Elinor Bergstein. Emile and Elinor wanted a through-line metaphor for the ultimate triumph of both Baby and Johnny. Once this lift was found we all knew its narrative power. I am not surprised as much as pleased when 'story' as the root of dance is proved so effective."[7] A reviewer (unable to find the name of the reviewer) wrote that the collaboration of the extremely talented artists on the movie: "shows you the possibilities of music, dance, love and the movies are endless, and it leaves you in a dream state, contemplating the beauty not only of the film's artistry, but of the human talent and drive that enabled it."

In closing, I think that what Mr. Swayze told the Telegraph.co.uk in 2006 ("Patrick Swayze on 'Dirty Dancing'") about why *Dirty Dancing* has been so successful is really the bottom-line: "It has been so successful because basically it's about love, and how the power of love can redeem us all."[8]

Credit: Vestron/The Kobal Collection at Art Resource, NY. Still taken from *Dirty Dancing*.

A defining moment in the film. Johnny (Patrick Swayze) has returned to Kellerman's and takes Baby out of the corner and up to the microphone. He says he is going to do the last dance his way, with Miss Frances Houseman (Baby, played by Jennifer Grey). Johnny stands up for Baby and himself, showing his respect for them and their relationship—in spite of what other people may think.

Credit: Vestron/The Kobal Collection at Art Resource, NY. Still taken from *Dirty Dancing*.

Johnny (Patrick Swayze) and Baby (Jennifer Grey) dance in the final scene of the movie. Their eyes reflect their heart and soul connection.

CHAPTER TWO

UPDATE ON THE *DIRTY DANCING* PHENOMENON: AUGUST 2010–APRIL 2013

The phenomenon of *Dirty Dancing* continues on its miraculous journey. The official *Dirty Dancing* Facebook page has over 15 million fans. There were multitudes of twenty-fifth anniversary screenings and celebrations of the movie all over the world in the summer of 2012. *Dirty Dancing* has impacted millions of people—not only fans watching the movie over and over again, but also those who have seen the stage show all over the world, who watched the 2010 *Dancing with the Stars* television show, who listened to the music in the original and updated versions, and who attended festivals. Need I also mention that there is quite a controversial remake in the works. Finally, a wax figure of Patrick Swayze as the character Johnny Castle from *Dirty Dancing* was unveiled in October 2011 at Madame Tussauds Hollywood.

Screenings, Festivals, and Events

I was fortunate to be one of hundreds and hundreds of people in attendance at an outdoor screening of the movie in July 2012 in Ann Arbor, Michigan. The experience was so much fun and so touching. It really made me miss Patrick Swayze even more and once again thank him for such a wonderful performance, and it also really brought back to me the popularity of this movie and how much of a classic this movie has turned into. Watching how many college students and fans of other ages—both male and female—were so into the movie was just mind-blowing.

The two main film locations—Mountain Lake Lodge (the new name for Mountain Lake Hotel) in Pembroke, Virginia, and Lake Lure in North Carolina—continue to be visited by scores of fans. In addition, beginning in 2010, there have been three annual *Dirty Dancing* festivals in Lake Lure. In the summer of 2012, a *Dirty Dancing* festival was started in Pearisburg, Virginia (near Mountain Lake Lodge). Finally, Mountain Lake Lodge continues to host *Dirty Dancing* weekends.

Dirty Dancing Stage Show

The *Dirty Dancing* stage show premiered in 2004 and has continued to be a smashing success throughout the world, with a current brand new tour in the United Kingdom slated to finish in January 2015. The millionth ticket for the United Kingdom and Ireland tour, which has been on the road for eighteen months, was sold on April 10, 2013. Tickets for the stage show can also be purchased for venues in Ireland, Hong Kong, and Singapore.

Both Josef Brown from Australia (who originated the role of Johnny Castle in the stage show) and Paul-Michael Jones from the United Kingdom (who plays Johnny Castle currently) have indicated that watching Patrick Swayze in *Dirty Dancing* gave them the okay to be both masculine and a dancer. In an August 24, 2012 article, "Still having the time of our lives at *Dirty Dancing*," David Henshall discusses this with Paul-Michael Jones:

> **[Jones] explains, he jumped at the chance to play the role, not least because Patrick Swayze, the original Johnny Castle, is one of his heroes.**
>
> **As a young dancer growing up in Rochdale, Swayze was a role model for him. His parents ran a dance school, and at age 11 he took up Latin and ballroom dancing.**

> **"*Dirty Dancing* was a great film for me to watch—seeing Patrick Swayze dancing and making it cool," he says. "I became a fan pretty quickly."**

Jones is further quoted as saying:

> **"The producers have purposely tried to make it as close as possible to the movie. As for Swayze himself, I didn't deliberately copy him while I was rehearsing but at the same time I didn't try to waver too far away from him because that's what the audience wants to see."[1]**

Credit: Alastair Muir. Courtesy of Target Live.

Jill Winterize as Baby and Paul-Michael Jones as Johnny in the UK Dirty Dancing *stage show.*

Credit: Alastair Muir. Courtesy of Target Live.

Nicky Griffiths as Penny and Paul-Michael Jones as Johnny in the UK Dirty Dancing *stage show.*

Jennifer Grey and *Dancing with the Stars*

On November 23, 2010, Jennifer Grey (who played the female lead character, Baby Houseman, in *Dirty Dancing*) and her professional dance partner, Derek Hough, were pronounced the winners on the television show *Dancing with the Stars*. The show had about 24 million viewers per episode and had many ties to *Dirty Dancing*. Grey and Hough danced to two songs from the movie—"These Arms of Mine" and "Do You Love Me?"—and Grey carried the watermelon again. It was widely reported in the media that, when dancing to these *Dirty Dancing* songs in rehearsals, Grey became very emotional about her past experiences with Patrick Swayze and missing him.

Grey was chosen as the person of the week for an ABC interview with Diane Sawyer on August 24, 2012, which coincided with the movie's twenty-fifth anniversary. Sawyer pointed out that Grey had not danced for almost twenty-five years due to self-doubt. Grey told Diane Sawyer about why she decided to compete on *Dancing with the Stars*:

> **. . . because Patrick had just passed and I had just had thyroid cancer . . . I was realizing, why am I not dancing? Why am I letting anything stand in the way of my joy?**

Grey also said:

> **I feel that thing, I think what people experience when they get older, of how precious and fragile this life is. I think you cannot be dancing and not be in joy.[2]**

In her April 29, 2010 article "*Dirty Dancing* Is The Greatest Movie Of All Time," Irin Carmon talks about how she spoke to Eleanor Bergstein that week about her creation of the character Baby Houseman:

> **In [Bergstein's] mind as in mine, Jennifer Grey's Baby is a strong-minded idealistic young woman with her own interests, who doesn't have to**

change herself to get the guy even as she undergoes a transformation from gawky wallflower to confident onstage dancer. . . .

[Bergstein says:] "I conceived of her and made her a fighter. A girl who just won't give up."[3]

The *Dirty Dancing* Soundtrack

On November 5, 2010, the Black Eyed Peas released the lead single "The Time (Dirty Bit)" from their new sixth studio album, *The Beginning*. "The Time (Dirty Bit)" uses part of the chorus of the *Dirty Dancing* song "(I've Had) The Time of My Life" (written by Franke Previte, Donald Markowitz, and John DeNicola and performed by Bill Medley and Jennifer Warnes) and became a smash hit in the United States and throughout the world. On November 23, 2010, the music video for "The Time (Dirty Bit)" was released; by April 2013, it had over 206 million views on YouTube.

On September 7, 2010, Franke Previte made the demos of "(I've Had) The Time of My Life" and "Hungry Eyes" (written by Franke Previte and John DeNicola) and "Someone Like You" (a song in the *Dirty Dancing* stage show) available for digital purchase, with the proceeds going to the Patrick Swayze Pancreas Cancer Research Fund at the Stanford Cancer Institute and the Pancreatic Cancer Action Network. In an August 8, 2011 Popdose interview by Rob Smith, Previte spoke about how he then re-issued three downloadable records from his 1980s band, Franke & the Knockouts, and a best hits album, *Sweetheart—Anniversary Edition*, to raise additional money for the above-mentioned pancreatic cancer funds. *Sweetheart—Anniversary Edition* includes the original version of "Hungry Eyes" and "Beat of a Broken Heart" (which was written by Previte over ten years ago, in case there would be a *Dirty Dancing 2*).

Smith: What brought up this whole reissue campaign? The stuff's been out of print for so long.

Previte: I was the writer of "(I've Had) The Time of My Life" and "Hungry Eyes," and those songs were, like, very close to Patrick Swayze when I met him at the Academy Awards [in 1988]. The story he told me was how they didn't have the final song for the last scene, and they were getting ready to film to a Lionel Richie track. They were like, it's a good song, but it's not an original song and it's not our song. They had listened to 149 songs up to that point. He said, "We got to the last tape and the 150th song we listened to was '(I've Had) The Time of My Life.' And we started screaming and we were thrilled with your demo." They filmed out of sequence, so they were doing the last scene first. He said, "By the time that take was over, we just looked at each other and said, 'Oh man, what just happened?' We knew we had a great movie, and the song just inspired us to do the rest of *Dirty Dancing*."

I'd spent some other time with Patrick at some other charity events, and I knew how special a person he was—there was a little Johnny Castle in Patrick, and vice versa.[4]

Regarding additional happenings with this iconic song, the *Glee* cast recorded "(I've Had) The Time of My Life" and performed it on their November 30, 2010 episode. In 2011, the song was also named the most-played romantic duet during the past ten years by PPL, a music licensing company in the United Kingdom.

Surprisingly, the soundtrack of *Dirty Dancing* pops up in a 2012 study as the most arousing music to play during sex among both female and male respondents. Spotify, a digital music service, commissioned the study to look at the relationship between music, romance, and seduction. Dr. Daniel Müllensiefen, a music psychologist, conducted the "Science Behind the Song" study, which included interviewing two thousand people in the United Kingdom between the ages of eighteen and ninety-one, with just about an equal number of men and women.

In honor of the twenty-fifth anniversary of the movie, *Dirty Dancing: The Deluxe Anniversary Edition* (with Mr. Jimmy Ienner, Executive Producer, RCA) was released in September 2012. It was dedicated to Patrick Swayze.

The *Dirty Dancing* Remake

In August 2011, it was announced that a *Dirty Dancing* remake was being done with Kenny Ortega as director. While Jennifer Grey spoke up in favor of the remake, tons of fans expressed disbelief and anger with this development. Originally, it was said that the release would be on July 26, 2013, but on June 8, 2012, it was postponed until at least 2014. The original writer of the remake was Maria Maggenti (*Monte Carlo*), and in April 2012, it was announced that Brad Falchuk (*Glee*) was replacing her.

The Patrick Swayze Statue at Madame Tussauds Hollywood

On a touching, bittersweet note, Lisa Niemi Swayze helped unveil the wax statue of Patrick Swayze at Madame Tussauds Hollywood on October 19, 2011. Swayze's wax figure is balancing on a log over a lake, as in the scene from *Dirty Dancing* in which Johnny teaches Baby the importance of balance in dance. Please see chapter four for the details, including my sentimental visit to this wonderful tribute to Swayze.

Dirty Dancing in Popular Culture

Regarding other cultural influences of *Dirty Dancing*, there were several that I have really enjoyed. There was a rumor on the Internet that Kate Middleton's sister, Pippa, was planning a *Dirty Dancing*–themed hen party at their family home to celebrate Kate's 2011 nuptials with Prince William.

There was controversy in August 2012 in Sweden because the famous *Dirty Dancing* line "Nobody puts Baby in a corner" was etched into the front of the new library at Karlstad University, and many people were not happy about this. In response to the criticism, Åsa Bergenheim, the university rector, stated that the quote was placed there to provide inspiration, and she was widely quoted in the media as saying: "It means that we straighten our backs and give our best—because we are capable."

Finally, the lift scene has been mimicked by so many people in so many settings, especially in movies and television shows. Two of my favorite re-enactments both include Channing Tatum: lifting his dog on *The Ellen DeGeneres Show* on February 8, 2012, and then lifting his wife (while "(I've Had) The Time of My Life" was playing) at the surprise, dancing flash mob party that she held for him on April 27, 2012 in honor of his thirty-second birthday. By the way, the media reports that, as Tatum was growing up, he considered Patrick Swayze to be a hero.

The *Dirty Dancing* Legacy

The *Dirty Dancing* phenomenon goes on and on, with no end in sight. I really look forward to all of the twists and turns it will take in the future.

I will end this chapter on the continuing popularity and legacy of *Dirty Dancing* with two quotes.

First, Mitchell Krugel, author of the 1988 book *PATRICK SWAYZE*, wrote this regarding Patrick Swayze:

> **As Johnny, he made Baby feel so good that she was scared of never feeling that way again. And he made his fans feel so good that they want to keep on feeling that way, even if they have to come back to the theater again and again to do so.[5]**

I think that the above statement has stood the test of time and will always be true—not just for theater showings of the movie, but also for anything to do with *Dirty Dancing*, such as the stage show and the music.

In her interview with Jennifer Grey in honor of the twenty-fifth anniversary of *Dirty Dancing*, Diane Sawyer commented about how three generations of women still get together to watch *Dirty Dancing*, "the unchanging human story from a simpler, more innocent time"; Jennifer Grey replied:

> **I think that people have a very, very tender spot for this movie. They project, you know, when everything was possible. When anything could happen . . .** [2]

CHAPTER THREE

LINDA GOTTLIEB

PRODUCER, *DIRTY DANCING*
New York City
November 17, 2012 (telephone interview)

How did you get involved with *Dirty Dancing*? Did you already know Eleanor Bergstein?

LINDA: I had known Eleanor Bergstein many years ago when we were both dating roommates, when we were very young, in our twenties. I had a job. I was the East Coast producer, the chief producer for MGM. I was working out of the MGM offices. My job was to come up with material that I would then produce. I was their sort of main person in the East Coast. So as part of that job, I constantly sought out writers. I mean, I was always looking for story material, movie material.

One day, Eleanor called me. She remembered me—had seen me being honored at a Women in Film lunch. She called and said, "You know, we used to know each other. I have some ideas for a film." So I took her to lunch at a restaurant called Between the Bread in New York. She sat down and she said, "Well, I want to do this film about two sisters in the Catskills. One of them is a natural dancer and it would involve Latin music." And *Tango Argentino* had just become a big success as a theatrical show in New York, and I thought, "Well, maybe there is something out there in the zeitgeist that says there's time for Latin music." I said, "Well, tell me the story."

"Well, I really don't have the story. I am interested in these two sisters."

And since I'm one of two sisters, as is Eleanor, that sort of interested me.

I said, "You don't have the story?"

"Well, no, not really. I just have the venue—the Catskills."

So I said, "Well, tell me about yourself. I don't really know your early background" (which I always ask writers).

She said, "I grew up in Brooklyn. My father was a doctor. You know, I was a natural dancer. I was one of those girls who used to go dirty dancing with the guys from the wrong side of the tracks."

And I literally dropped my spoon and said, "That is a million-dollar title!"

She said, "What is?"

I said, "*Dirty Dancing*."

She said, "But that has nothing to do with the story I want to tell."

I said, "Eleanor, that's the title, and now we're going to get the story."

So at lunch that day, we invented the character of Johnny over this lunch at Between the Bread. In other words, it was not ever in her original thinking, but it came from the title of *Dirty Dancing*.

I said, "You know, if there's dirty dancing, what's the other kind of music?"

She said, "You know, it's clean teen music." And we realized that there was a musical clash between the clean teen music—["Big Girls Don't Cry"], which begins the movie—and the dirty dancing music, which of course you know very well. So Johnny was born at lunch.

I love it.

LINDA: I said, "Let's pitch this." That was my job. I took it in as a producer to MGM. And MGM said they wanted to go ahead and develop it, which meant that they funded the cost of the script—you know, the first draft, the second draft script—which Eleanor developed with me, which I was totally involved in the development of that script. When the script came in and we finally turned it in to MGM, the head of MGM soon after that time—the guy who had hired me and who believed in me, a man named Frank Yablans—was fired. When he was fired, all his projects went into turnaround. Do you know what that means?

No.

LINDA: The turnaround means the studio who financed it gives the rights back for a year to the producer—to me. I controlled the rights for a year. I had one year to set it up elsewhere and pay them back the money or otherwise the rights reverted back to MGM and it was all over. So I had one year to kind of figure out how to get *Dirty Dancing* made. I had seven other projects in the same position, but *Dirty Dancing* was the one I was going to focus on. So that's sort of the story of how it went from MGM through me. We had no cast or anything. I then took it and shopped it around to every major studio—all who turned it down. I think I had something like forty-three rejections. I mean, I looked everywhere. Nobody wanted to make that movie. I was trying to raise independent money to do it.

A little company called Vestron called through my agent. My agent called me and said, "Somebody wants to make the movie." I thought it was a crank phone call. I had been turned down so many times. Vestron said they were interested in meeting with me about producing it. There are two people there, Mitchell Cannold and Steve Reuther. Mitchell himself had grown up in the Catskills, and so the story resonated for him, and he was a big fan of it. They took the title of executive producers on the movie, and basically came up with the financing, provided that I could figure out a way to do the movie for under $5 million—for about $4.5 million—which was very hard to do, but we did.

I mean, we made it in a right-to-work state. We couldn't shoot in the real Catskills because, first of all, they didn't look the same. The Catskills now don't look like the Catskills of the 1960s. So we had to re-create them, and we realized it was cheaper to go down to Virginia and North Carolina, which were non-union states. We could shoot more cheaply—extras were cheaper. So we re-created the Catskills in sort of the Bible-Belt South.

So what was the casting process like—for Baby and Johnny?

LINDA: We began looking for the two leads. The first person that we saw was Jennifer. I had known of her—somebody had suggested her to me. I had seen her in *Ferris Bueller* and I thought, "I don't know, that's kind of weird." But I knew her family, actually. My kids had gone to school with her brother. I knew Joel. And so she came; she was the first person who walked in the door. Her father, Joel Grey, was there, and he sort of pushed her forward. She was stammering and scared. And the first audition was just dancing. All we wanted to do was just turn on some music and let's see how you move. She clearly moved well. She's a good dancer.

And then she stopped dancing and she turned to us—the director, myself, and Eleanor. And she said (I'm winging this, but she said something like), "I just have to say something. I know I shouldn't, but I have to say something. I'm just like this girl, Baby. I talk too much. I care too much about everything I do. I so understand this girl. I'm exactly like her." And then she said, "Oh, I shouldn't have said it. Oh, forget I said that." And of course, we fell in love with her. And then we saw, you know, 150 other girls and then we cast Jennifer. She was the first person we saw.

As to Patrick, I had known about Patrick some years ago because I had been working in the industry and had been thinking about doing a film involving ballet (which, for various reasons, I didn't do). In the course of the research as to who could play the lead in that film, I had discovered that Patrick had been trained as a classical ballet dancer.

So I suggested him to our casting agent, Bonnie Timmermann. We brought him in. We screened everything he had done. We brought him in, and we, of course, loved him. But the question was, was he too old? I mean, at the time, Patrick was thirty-seven; Jennifer was twenty-seven. They both looked much younger. But how would that play on screen?

And for Patrick, of course he could dance, but he did not know how to do dirty dancing at all. He was overly trained as a ballet dancer. And so, for him, it was a process of unlearning a lot of that and sort of getting groovy—getting into his body in a different way. Kenny Ortega was great, you know, training him and working with him and loosening him up. It wasn't where his training had been.

We did a screen test of Jennifer and Patrick, and a screen test of Billy Zane and Kyra Sedgwick. They were the alternative couple. And of course, the rest is history.

Yeah. Wow. What do you think are your fondest memories of filming *Dirty Dancing*?

LINDA: The actual making of *Dirty Dancing* was a nightmare. It was horribly difficult, so the things that I remember the most are the catastrophes—which I'm sure you read about in the *Huffington Post* ["'Dirty Dancing' Turns 25: The Blockbuster Film That Almost Wasn't Made," by Laura Rowley, August 26, 2012].

We didn't even start shooting until (as I recall) August. We were shooting in the South. So after continuing to shoot the supposed summer, the trees started to change. You know, we were shooting in late September—I think we started in September—so the trees were changing. I remember, "Oh my God, what are we going to do? The leaves aren't matching." So we ended up spray-painting the leaves to keep them looking like summer. We armed our department with spray cans.

It became so cold that [in] the famous lift-in-the-lake scene, where she's doing the lift in the lake, Jennifer was freezing.

Do you recall which location that was at? Was it Virginia or North Carolina, or both?

LINDA: That was in Blacksburg, Virginia, where the water was. . . . In Lake Lure, we did the interiors. We did the balancing on the log. We did the interior of the staff quarters and then, you know, we had to match everything, of course, to look like the hotel in Blacksburg. So I remember those catastrophes. I remember things like, you know, Patrick falling off the log. I'm sure you know about those stories, right?

Yes.

LINDA: You know, my taking him to the emergency room, having them drain his knee. He never wanted a stunt double. You know these stories. He didn't want a stunt double. He insisted on doing his stunts all himself, which always irritated everybody else, frankly, because he was fragile—his knees were fragile. He had been hurt as a dancer. It was a very macho thing for him. He didn't want anybody doing his stunts.

So Jennifer had . . .

LINDA: Oh, yeah. She had a stunt double—the whole thing where she's going across the log—if you can notice, that's a stunt double. She was properly cautious. Patrick had to do that himself. He was a wild guy—you know, a guy's guy. So he had to do all that.

You know, certainly at the beginning of the film, they were not the best of friends. They had worked together in *Red Dawn*. They certainly admired each other's works. You know, all that chemistry that everybody talks about certainly wasn't on the set.

Did they get to become friends later on?

LINDA: I think they became friends, but when you make a movie, it's really hard. Tensions are high. They were very different. Patrick was a trained dancer. He understood discipline. If you did ten takes with Patrick, they would be pretty much the same. If you did ten takes with Jennifer, they'd be wildly different because she was, first of all, not trained. She didn't have the technique. He could summon up technique. He understood technique. Jennifer was intuitive, volatile—you know, she would cry easily. She's great, I mean, I'm crazy about her—absolutely love her—but she was unpredictable and that sort of annoyed Patrick—you know, that you'd never get the same thing twice. She would sometimes be impatient. At the time, I think she was dating Matthew Broderick.

It was a hard time. It was a hard shoot. It was very hot and difficult conditions—you know, working in extreme heat—with dancing scenes with hot lights and all that. It was a really difficult shoot.

She was in every scene or almost every scene.

LINDA: She was in almost every scene, yeah.

So the memories of it that I have are, you know, the producer's memories. I tell you, actually, one of the most wonderful things was the stuff that they improvised—like the Sylvia and Mickey song, which was all improvised by the director on the set. And those moments which were not scripted, which they came up with, were so wonderful and so surprising.

Even that montage of her learning—running up and down the steps. That was a wonderful surprise which came about because we didn't have enough wardrobe for her. We had such a limited budget. The wardrobe costume person just came in, and I said, "We want to do a whole montage for learning to dance—for practicing." She comes in with two or three changes.

I said, "What is this, Hilary? Where's the wardrobe?"

"This is what I have. I didn't have any more money."

So we were in a complete pickle in the editing room—how to show that. The director had this brilliant idea of getting the Surfaris song "Wipe Out" and step-printing it. So if you look at that whole montage of her going up and down the steps, she is wearing the same two things or three things. It's just a way of covering up the fact that we really couldn't show—usually you show passage of time with a lot of different wardrobe changes, and we didn't have them. So necessity was definitely the mother of invention.

Wow. That's just so amazing—how it came out in the end.

LINDA: It's always in the editing room where you figure it out. You figure out what works, what doesn't work.

I think Patrick is definitely the heartthrob of this movie—what many people remember. But I do think it's Baby, the character Baby, that makes people enter the movie. For women, particularly. Women feel that they can identify with her because she's less than perfect. She's not a stunning beauty or anything. She's flawed the way most of us are flawed. She's insecure. And if she can get the guy because of her inner beauty, I think it gives hope to girls and women who are looking at that movie. I think that's the fairy tale aspect of it. So the casting, I think, was just a happy, happy perfection, really—the two of them. I mean, imagine Patrick with a gorgeous girl, with a knockout teenage beauty. It doesn't play as well. I don't think. I don't know if you agree.

I think so. I had read that there had been thoughts from Patrick that maybe Penny and Johnny should, you know, be together.

LINDA: He definitely thought that. First of all, he wanted his wife to play Penny.

That's what I was going to say next. Yeah.

LINDA: He pitched that and we looked at her. We considered her. We just thought that she wasn't as strong as Cynthia Rhodes. You know, he understood the decision. Then, he had (the way actors often do) his opinions as to where the script should be. So that was it. I mean actors do—are entitled to [opinions], but we really felt that it should go the other way, and history proved us quite right.

Yes, absolutely. So, any other stories about Patrick Swayze—what it was like to work with him?

LINDA: . . . He was not a morning person. So, really, there were people assigned to just literally get him out of bed, get him to the set on time. Once he was there, he was a total professional. He was a guy who liked to ride his motorcycle, and we wouldn't let him do that sometimes. He was such a sweet guy. He had such a sweet heart, a really good heart. If he liked you, you were his buddy, you know, you were his friend. He really was never mean to people. He was a very, very kind man. I saw him years later, you know, and very warm, very loving embrace. He loved animals. He was happiest, I think, back at his ranch. He would want that. He kept to himself. He was a good guy.

I don't know what else I can tell you. Originally, we shot some nude footage for it. We did some sort of bare-breasted stuff with Jennifer, which the studio wanted for awhile, and then they changed their minds, and I think I was glad that they did. It was really a much better film as a PG-13 film, you know, getting younger kids.

It was the only film, I think, in its original version, it got an R rating from the Rating Board. I appealed it. I said, "Why? It has no nudity. Why did you give us an R rating? We protest."

The head of the Rating Board (who was actually a former boss of mine, Dick Heffner) said to me, "Well, everyone just felt it was such a sexy film." It's interesting, you know.

So I said, "Yeah, but it's sexy because dance is sexy, but really we've done nothing explicit here."

So we had one of those negotiations: "If you take out two *shit*s and a whatever, you know, a couple of swear words in it, we'll go back and reconsider it."

So we edited out a couple of curses, and they gave us a PG-13. It was interesting because everybody felt its sensuality. It is a film nowadays where you can see everything on camera, everything on the screen. This was a film that had nothing explicit, and it was so clearly a turn-on movie, a sexy movie, because dance is sexy. You know, if you do it, shoot it right.

Emile understood it. I hired him—Emile Ardolino—because he understood the power of dance, and he knew how to shoot dance. Which every other director I had talked to—I felt they understood the drama, but that they really didn't get . . . the centrality of dance to these characters and to the film. He had directed a movie called *He Makes Me Feel Like Dancin'*, which won the Academy Award, which was terrific. We hired him on the basis that he had never done a feature before, so it was quite a risk. The whole movie was a risk, a risk that would never be taken today—this film would never be made today. You know this era of films—of vampire movies—it just wouldn't have gotten made. Well, and it almost didn't get made.

You're in the movie. Is that what I read in the interview [in the *Huffington Post*]?

LINDA: You know, we were shooting down South and we clearly had to have Jewish-looking extras or people who looked reasonably like they could have been in the Catskills. So we put out a casting call, for—what did we say, "ethnic types"? You know you can't really say. And of course all these people appeared who were blonde and blue-eyed with string ties and didn't look like they had anything to do with being in the Catskills.

So I sort of pressed anybody—myself included—into service more prominently. So I did [appear] in the film when they're unloading the car—I had a brief starring appearance. You blink and you miss me—in a backless dress, a white cotton dress that's white with blue turquoise sort of stripes and a full skirt, getting luggage out of a car. A couple of our other people: Eleanor's in the dance sequence, my sister came down to visit and was in the dance sequence, my kids were. You know, we were sort of desperate for people who looked reasonably like they should be there.

You do know the story of how we replaced the Bungalow Bunny with Miranda?

Yeah.

LINDA: That's a really hilarious story. The moments I remember are those disasters. The first day of shooting with five hundred extras when the director said to me, the woman we had cast to play the mother, she said, "No way." She was feeling sick. She had to have seven meals a day. It was just going to be a disaster, so we basically let her go and re-cast the mother in a hurry. Kelly Bishop was supposed to play the other part—the sexy woman, Vivian Pressman—but we needed a mother. We were there with five hundred extras and we had just lost the other woman. We said, "Kelly."

The director looked at me, and he said, "Go over and stand next to Jerry Orbach. Come here, Jennifer. Sit next to them." He looked at me. "It looks like a family to me."

I said, "It looks perfect to me, Emile."

I said [to Kelly], "Would you mind playing a different part than what you thought you were playing?"

She said, "No, I'll do whatever you want me to do." She became the mother by accident.

Then we needed to get another Vivian Pressman. So we brought in one person we flew in from New York, and we tried her out, and we were not happy. All of a sudden, Miranda Garrison, who was the assistant choreographer, knocked on my door, and she comes in, and I said, "Oh, hi, Miranda. How come you're all dressed up with your hair piled on top of your head and your skirt up to your crotch?"

She said, "Well, I hear you have an opening."

"But Miranda, you're the assistant choreographer."

She said, "But I have my SAG card."

I said, "Okay, read for the part," and she was terrific.

It was like this chain reaction of casting. We did everything quote wrong unquote. You don't do that. You don't re-cast like that when you're shooting. We did it all wrong, but it turned out happily.

It sure did. So that comes to, you know, over twenty-five years, and it's still going strong.

LINDA: Yep. Of course, now they're doing a remake of it.

Well, I didn't know if I should bring that up or not.

LINDA: You can bring it up, sure. We're not involved. None of us is involved in it.

I don't get it.

LINDA: I don't get it, either. I'm going to be very interested to see what they do and how faithfully they shoot to the original. What do you think the reaction would be, Sue?

Horrible. Horrible. None of the fans want it. They're very upset—especially regarding Patrick . . . well, he's been gone about three years. They feel it's like a slap in the face to him.

LINDA: Look, they made that prequel, *Havana Nights*, which was just awful.

Yeah.

LINDA: Again, they didn't go to any of the people who originally made the film. Then they did a television series—again, without coming back to any of the original players—and that failed. And now they're doing a remake. I don't know, I mean, we'll see.

Kenny Ortega is the director. I read somewhere that Jennifer was all for it. Then I read somewhere that Patrick's wife, Lisa, was all for it. What was she going to say? I don't think she knew about it ahead of time. I don't see how it's going to work.

LINDA: It seems surprising to me, but, you know, they are talking about some big names in it. Who knows? I think usually those things work better when it's not a good film—when you remake something that's a less-than-perfect thing or needs updating. I can't imagine updating that story. None of us has seen a script. We'll see.

They've already delayed it.

LINDA: Yeah, well, because the first person hired to write the script was somebody I knew. Apparently, that didn't work. They have another writer on it now, somebody from *Glee*.

So it seems like they're shooting for a young population, a young demographic to watch it.

LINDA: I think you're right.

None of the fans want it. Reading Facebook and, you know, the various articles on the Internet, and talking to people (especially Patrick's fan club members), nobody's for it—none of the fans I mean. So it would have to be for the younger demographic.

For my first book, I had interviewed a gal, she was only seventeen then, and another gal was in her twenties—but these people started watching the movie when they were very young. One of them was six.

LINDA: Yeah, the film has had, like, three different whole generations of people, which is so interesting. It's just as popular today. It ages very well, which, you know, is not always the case. It's interesting because there have been other films of dance that just haven't lasted, whether it's *Flashdance* or you name it. They haven't had the currency, but I think [*Dirty Dancing* does] because it's really emotionally true. It's a fairy tale, a grounded fairy tale.

And it's also interesting because it's about class—very few films are, in America. The obstacle to their love affair is really that he's lower class and that her father doesn't like that. And yet his supposed Jewish principles are that everyone is the same, and Baby calls him on it. So it has a real moral heart to it, which I think gives it part of its strength also.

Thank you so much for the interview.

DANCING FILM PRODUCTIONS, INC.

c/o Mountain Lake Hotel
Route 1, P.O. Box 105B
Pembroke, VA 24136
703/626-7251

MOUNTAIN LAKE GUEST LIST

1. Emile Ardolino
2. Linda Gottlieb
3. Eleanor Bergstein
4. Doro Bachrach
5. Curtis Pepper
6. Jennifer Grey
7. Patrick Swayze
8. Cynthia Rhodes
9. Jane Brucker - from 9/3
10. Jerry Orbach - from 9/3
11. Neal Jones - from 9/4
12. Lynne Lipton - from 9/4
13. Jack Weston - from 9/4
14. "Stan" - from 9/4 - approx. 9/5 (lv. 9/6)
15. Paula Truman - from 9/4 - approx. 9/11 (lv. 9/12)
16. Alvin Myerovich - from 9/4 - approx. 9/11 (lv. 9/12)
17. Antone Pagan - from 9/8 - approx. 9/9 (lv. 9/10)
18. Kelly Bishop - from 9/10 - approx. 9/12 (lv. 9/13)
19. Lonny Price - from 9/6
20. Adger Cowans - from 9/3
21. Mark Haack
22. Marilyn Bailes
23. Tom Allen
24. Hilary Rosenfeld
25. Claudia Anderson
26. Lisa Feldbauer
27. Mark Burchard
28. Steve Lineweaver
29. Kenny Ortega
30. Miranda Garrison
31. Julia Cort - from 9/3
32. Susan Pickett - from 9/2
33. Jennifer Gilbert
34. Mike Barrow
35. John Merriman - from 9/2 or 9/3
36. Quintin Woo - from 9/3
37. Scott Zigler - from 9/3
38. Greg White-Wiegand - 9/3
39. Donne Daniels
40. Peter Van Eynde - from 9/4
41. Bill Flick - from 9/3 or 9/4
42. Michael Sudmier - from 9/3 or 9/4
43. Marlies Vallant
44. Frida Arnadottir
45. Jimi White
46. Jeanie D'Iorio
47. Isabelle Cramer
48. Sabrina Padwa
49. Jacob Conrad
50. Neil Holcomb

Courtesy of Mountain Lake Hotel.

Taken inside of Madame Tussauds. Image shown depicts wax figure created and owned by Madame Tussauds.

Lisa Niemi Swayze participated in the unveiling of a wax figure of Patrick Swayze on October 19, 2011 at Madame Tussauds Hollywood.

CHAPTER FOUR

PATRICK SWAYZE'S STATUE AT MADAME TUSSAUDS HOLLYWOOD

LISA NIEMI SWAYZE UNVEILS PATRICK'S WAX STATUE

The *Daily Mail* quotes Lisa Niemi Swayze during her participation in the unveiling of Patrick's statue on October 19, 2011, in an article by Mike Larkin on that same date.

> **And she said the finished work is striking an appropriate pose for her late husband.**
>
> **She said: "(He is saying) come and be fearless with me.**
>
> **Go out on a limb. Just trust. Don't look down. Take a chance in whatever you do."[1]**

Multiple media sources reported that Lisa found the experience to be bittersweet.

MADAME TUSSAUDS STAFF INTERVIEW
September 14, 2012 (email interview)

A special thank you to Rowena Adalid, Head of Marketing, Madame Tussauds Hollywood, who compiled the answers.

Who decided to make a statue of Patrick? Is there a committee who nominates and then votes for various stars?

Madame Tussauds chooses figures based on our guests' feedback and suggestions. *Dirty Dancing* is such an iconic film and Patrick Swayze was a highly requested figure, so it was just an obvious choice for the Hollywood location.

Why was this particular scene from *Dirty Dancing* chosen for the statue?

There were several scenes considered, but the log scene was chosen because it is very interactive. It gives our guests a chance to step onto the log, stare at Patrick Swayze's eyes, recreate that moment in the film, and dance with him. It is a total immersive experience that you cannot do anywhere else.

How long did it take to make the statue, and how many people were involved in making it?

A team of twenty artists over four months at a cost of $300,000.

Was it an emotional experience for the people on the team making the statue, and had any of the team met Patrick or Lisa (Patrick's wife)?

It was definitely an emotional experience for everyone involved, as we decided to make the figure posthumously. Lisa was very involved throughout the entire process, and we are very lucky to have had her involvement as she served as our artists' guide.

What was the hardest part about making the statue?

Making sure that the finished product is what Patrick wants it to be if he was alive. He is also a dancer, so it is not just getting his face exactly right, but also making sure that the wax figure body is positioned like a dancer would hold himself up on a log, so a lot of effort was made in achieving this.

How much of a role did Lisa have in the creation of the statue?

Lisa was highly involved in the project, and we truly valued her support throughout the figure-making process. We wanted to ensure that, for his fans and also fans of the film, that we create a fantastic and accurate figure, and the results speak for themselves, so we are really grateful for Lisa's participation.

What kind of feedback have the fans given about Patrick's statue?

Fans love the figure. The response is very positive, and we received a lot of messages thanking us for honoring Patrick Swayze in this special way because they all agree that he deserves a wax figure at Madame Tussauds.

Is this the only statue of Patrick in any of the Madame Tussauds wax museums?

Yes.

Note: Ms. Adalid shared that all of the Madame Tussauds figures are created by Madame Tussauds artists in London.

Taken inside of Madame Tussauds. Image shown depicts wax figure created and owned by Madame Tussauds.

Kenny Ortega, choreographer, at the unveiling of Patrick Swayze's Dirty Dancing *wax figure at Madame Tussauds Hollywood.*

Taken inside of Madame Tussauds. Image shown depicts wax figure created and owned by Madame Tussauds.

Me and Patrick Swayze's wax figure during my awesome visit to Madame Tussauds Hollywood on December 23, 2012.

MY VISIT TO PATRICK'S MADAME TUSSAUDS HOLLYWOOD *DIRTY DANCING* STATUE
December 23, 2012

The big moment was finally here. I had been waiting since May to visit the museum to see Patrick's statue.

I stood in a short line to buy my ticket. The salesperson said that if I bought a program to the museum, it would lower my admission fee. I asked if Patrick was in the program, and she said she thought so. Of course, I bought the program.

I excitedly and somewhat impatiently waited until it was my turn to have my souvenir photo taken by a Madame Tussauds staff member, and then I would be free to do what I had come to do. I asked, "Where can I find Patrick Swayze's statue?" I was told to go to the second floor. As you can imagine, I very quickly figured out how to get to the second floor (which was not accessible by elevator).

First, I saw Tom Hanks (i.e., Forrest Gump) sitting on the bench with his suitcase, and then I rounded the corner and saw Dustin Hoffman (i.e., Benjamin in *The Graduate*), and then all of a sudden I saw straight ahead of me: Patrick's statue! It was positioned right next to Sylvester Stallone from *Rocky* and kitty-corner to the *Star Trek* figures. I just stopped in my tracks and stared. I knew right away that this was a huge and so well-deserved tribute to Patrick. What great company he was in with this location in the museum with all of these wonderful stars.

The statue of Patrick as the character Johnny in *Dirty Dancing* was so true to life. I felt overcome with emotion: if only Patrick were really still here. I could only speculate that somehow Patrick knew about his statue and enjoyed it.

I watched women and men and kids all try to balance on the log with Patrick—some succeeding and some not, but all posing with him for pictures. Of course, I had my own picture taken as well, by another visitor. Almost every person who came into the room stopped and took notice of Patrick's statue.

It seemed that this balancing on-the-log scene was a really wonderful choice from *Dirty Dancing* because, in addition to the fact that it is an interactive experience for visitors (as mentioned by Madame Tussauds staff), Patrick is surrounded by trees and nature—which he loved—and is doing what he loved: meeting a challenge and utilizing his natural dancing/athletic grace and ability.

I took this opportunity to enjoy this tribute to Patrick and also to say what I wanted to say to Patrick. I thanked him for all that he was still doing for me by his portrayal of the character Johnny and, most important, by the way he lived his life with boundless passion, spirit, courage, and dignity, which serves as great inspiration to me.

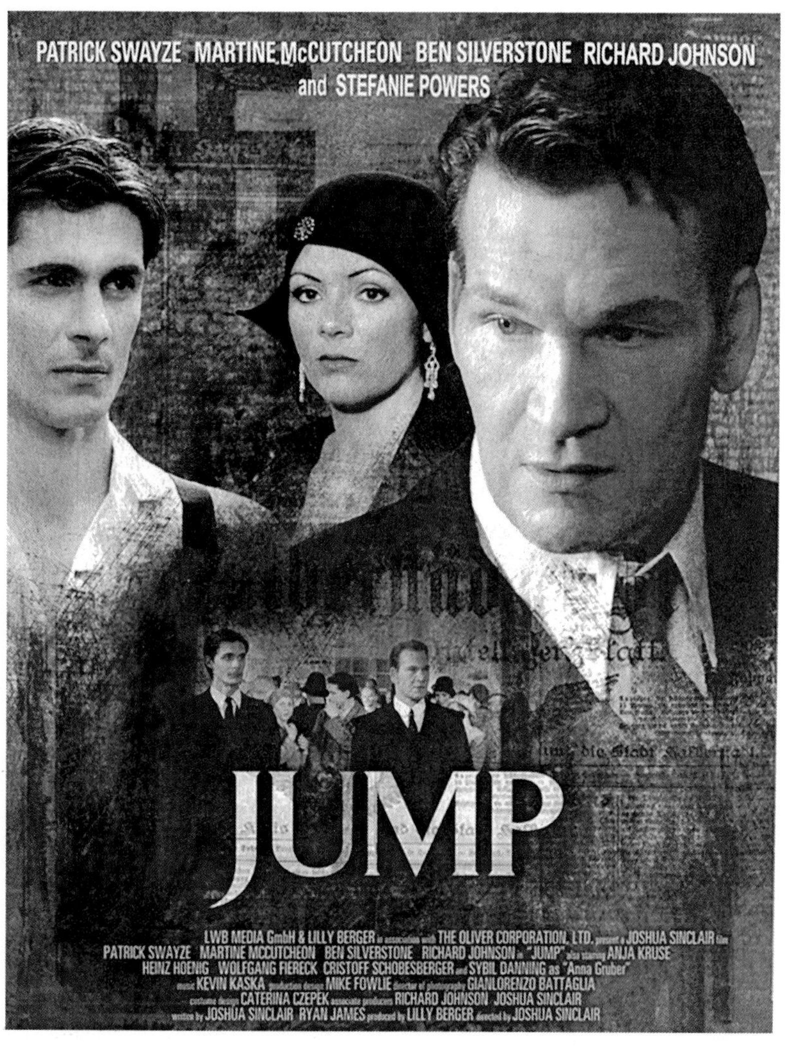

Used with permission of Joshua Sinclair.

On May 16, 2009, Patrick Swayze was awarded Best International Actor for his portrayal of Richard Pressburger in the 2008 Joshua Sinclair movie, Jump! *The true story of the acclaimed celebrity photographer Phillippe Halsman is told with the focus on his murder trial in 1928 in Austria. Patrick plays the attorney who helps Phillippe Halsman fight against the rampant anti-Semitism of the time.*

CHAPTER FIVE

TRIBUTE TO PATRICK SWAYZE

BY JOSHUA SINCLAIR

I have been fortunate enough to work with many wonderful filmmakers in my career. Some you may have heard of, others not. But they are all exceptional and timeless in their art. Vittorio De Sica, Sofia Loren, Roberto Rossellini and young Isabella, Richard Burton, Romy Schneider, Richard Harris, Trevor Howard, Kim Novak, Marlene Dietrich, David Bowie, Sean Penn, Martin Sheen, Karen Allen, Grace Jones, and even Tony Curtis at the end of his Billy Wilder heyday. And I am not just name-dropping unless it is to drop this one name: Patrick Swayze. Patrick was Truth. The cowboy's need to survive at its purest. There was always palpable truth in his emotions even against the backdrop of Hollywood's lies, deceptions, hypocrisy and false myths. Patrick was and will remain forever a genuine myth because he represented the humanity inherent in show business distilled to its essence.

In all my career, I have never met such a dedicated and passionate human being—on and off the set. And that is refreshing to say the least. Patrick Swayze was that sort of miracle that comes along only once or twice in any given generation. It was my privilege to have loved him, to still love him now. Oscar Wilde once said that we are all in the sewer but some of us are looking at the stars. Patrick was always looking at the stars, no matter what cards life had dealt him. And for that, I thank you Patrick—for your inspiration, for being a hymn to life. Some say we have lost Patrick. I say, no we haven't. I know exactly where he is.

Used with permission of Maurice Williams.

Maurice Williams, writer and performer of the iconic song "Stay."

CHAPTER SIX

MAURICE WILLIAMS

WRITER, SINGER/PERFORMER: MAURICE WILLIAMS & THE ZODIACS OF "STAY"
Charlotte, North Carolina
July 17, 2012 (telephone interview)

How did your song "Stay" get put in the movie? How did you get involved with *Dirty Dancing*?

MAURICE: The writer, Eleanor Bergstein, fought to get it in there.

She fought to get "Stay" in the movie?

MAURICE: Yes, and thought it was very fitting for the movie.

Wow. I noticed that so many different people have recorded your song "Stay"—like The Four Seasons, Jackson Browne, The Hollies. How do you feel when that happens?

MAURICE: It's fantastic. It's a blessing.

Is there anything you can tell me about when you wrote "Stay"? Was there any particular motivation for the song?

MAURICE: It was about a girl I was dating—trying to get her to stay longer on our date. Our families were friends. The girl was over at my parents' house. I was very young—like about fourteen to eighteen, somewhere in there. She had to go home. Her brother was going to pick her up at ten o'clock. I wanted her to stay a little longer, so I asked her could she stay a little longer, but she had to go anyway. So I wrote a song about it the next morning.

Oh, wow. That was pretty young to write such an awesome song. Had you been doing a lot of writing of other songs?

MAURICE: I also wrote "Little Darlin'." I was thirteen.

No, you weren't. Age thirteen?

MAURICE: Yes.

You were a prodigy. You were a child genius.

MAURICE: No, just regular.

Does that run in your family? Are there a lot of musicians?

MAURICE: No, I'm the only one. My sister—but she passed away . . .

I'm sorry.

MAURICE: . . . she played piano also, but she played classical piano. I play by ear. I hear it and I play it. My mother used to sing in the choir. That was about all. One sister can't sing at all.

Have you been surprised that *Dirty Dancing* has been so popular? It's almost twenty-five years old.

MAURICE: Yeah, gee whiz, what a thing that's going on. Everybody and their baby has seen the movie. Everybody has seen it. Some girls say they've watched it about twenty times. It's the story that it is, lasting . . . I think, because of the fact that it says so much for the underdog. There are a lot of guys like Patrick Swayze—the kid that he played in the movie, you know—the character. They were working these big country club places and resorts and they were the underdog and they would get blamed for everything. They just thought they were hired help. That happens for real—you know that goes on. I've even seen it in some of the places that we play.

Really.

MAURICE: I think everybody likes to see an underdog win in the case of that story. He came out a winner with the dances and everything and the girl. I think all that meant so much to people. Nobody is rich like that—well there are people—but they put themselves in that spot. Everybody works. They like to see winners win. I think that's the staying power, too. And of course, the music. The music—ooh, the music was fantastic.

So Eleanor did a good job of selecting. Was she the one who chose most of the music?

MAURICE: I don't know if she chose most of it. I think she was about fifty-fifty.

Oh, okay.

MAURICE: I think now—I'm not sure. She didn't tell me that. We met. She came down and presented me with a platinum album when the movie had sold so many millions. She came down and we talked—we talked forever. She's a nice lady and she told me all these things and all that good stuff. Quite a lady!

Oh, wow! It's just amazing to me how popular it is. And then now, you know, they're talking about the remake, but I guess it's been postponed.

MAURICE: They did a remake of it.

***Havana Nights*, you mean?**

MAURICE: They did another *Dirty Dancing*. I didn't dig it. It wasn't that good. It's hard to copy a movie like that. You know, it's just hard.

All the millions of shows and everything and everybody has seen it and you try to make another one. It's really hard to do.

Kenny Ortega, the choreographer of the original, has signed on to be the director of the remake that was supposed to come out in 2013. And then they said it has now been postponed until at least 2014 because of casting problems.

MAURICE: Oh, I see.

A lot of the fans were very upset to hear about another remake. "We're not going to go see that."

MAURICE: I understand. There's nothing wrong with the old one. It's something else.

About a week and a half ago, on a Sunday night, they [the Ann Arbor Summer Festival], showed *Dirty Dancing* outside on the college campus at the University of Michigan in Ann Arbor, and I went. There were hundreds and hundreds of people sitting in chairs or on the grass—yelling out the lines, dancing, things like that. I mean it's just so amazing.

MAURICE: Uh-huh.

Do you still perform? Do you still give concerts?

MAURICE: Yes, I do. I am semi-retired. I do a lot of doo-wop shows all over the country. We do those. It's very beautiful. There's nothing hard about it. They fly us from here to L.A. to do a show. I sing about three songs. There's a lot of energy. We talk about the movie and different things.

Oh, I am so glad. Do you ever come to Michigan?

MAURICE: Wasn't too long ago. It wasn't Detroit. We were up that way the weekend of April 20—like twenty to thirty miles outside of Detroit.

Wow. I'm sorry I missed that.

MAURICE: I can dig it.

Is there anything else you want to say about the movie?

MAURICE: I am sort of blessed to have a song in the movie that is such a classic and goes on forever. I hope it goes on forever, and it has.

Yes, it has. It's just so amazing.

MAURICE: It is—it really is.

I totally agree with you about the music in the movie. I mean, it is just incredible. I'm just so thrilled to talk to you.

MAURICE: It was my pleasure.

EXCERPTS FROM MAURICE WILLIAMS & THE ZODIACS DISCOGRAPHY[1*]

Maurice Williams was born in Lancaster, South Carolina in 1940. At a very young age he started singing in the choir at First Washington Baptist Church. . . . At age 12, Maurice sang with his first gospel group, The Jr. Harmonizers.

The Gladiolas' name [the first band that Maurice formed] was changed to Maurice Williams & The Zodiacs and in 1960 in Columbus, SC they recorded Maurice's song "Stay." It was released on the Herald label and went to number one on the national charts where it "stayed" that entire summer. The success of "Stay" and appearances on national TV shows like *The Merv Griffin Show* and *American Bandstand* established Maurice Williams & The Zodiacs as one of the hottest performing groups in the country. "To this day," says Maurice, "when I hear Mr. Henry (Shane) Gaston wail the high part, I still get the chills."

In 1987, Maurice Williams & The Zodiacs' version of "Stay" was used in the soundtrack of the popular movie "*Dirty Dancing*." In 1988, Maurice was presented with a Multi-Platinum Award for sales of more than 8,000,000 copies of its RCA Records soundtrack albums and cassettes.

Since 1957, Maurice Williams and his groups have performed in virtually every part of the country, sharing the bill with such top stars as Johnny Mathis, Jackson Browne, Diana Ross, Chubby Checker, The Kingston Trio, Alabama, Patti Labelle, Chuck Berry, James Brown, The Drifters, The Tams, Gladys Knight, Smokey Robinson, The Four Tops—and the list goes on.

In 1999, Maurice was part of the TNT network special, *Rock & Roll Graffiti* which reunited many classic artists. . . . May 2000 found the group in Pittsburgh filming the now classic *Doo-Wop 51* TV show.

Recognition continues to come Maurice Williams' way. A few years back, he received a commendation from the South Carolina

State legislature for his contributions to music. In 1999, Maurice was inducted into the South Carolina Music and Entertainment Hall of Fame. In 2001, South Carolina Governor Jim Hodges presented native son Maurice Williams with the state's highest civilian award, The Order of the Palmetto. Awarded the Hennessy Privilege Award in 2004, presented by Lieutenant Governor Andre Bauer of South Carolina, and Noel Hankin; and the Bill Pinkney Legend Award in Columbia, SC.

***Special thanks to Maurice Williams for permission to use excerpts from his discography.**

Courtesy of Jackie Horner.

Jackie Horner, Van Johnson, and Lou Goldstein at Grossinger's, summer of 1963.

CHAPTER SEVEN

JACKIE HORNER

STORY CONSULTANT FOR *DIRTY DANCING*
Liberty, New York
June 17, 2012 (telephone interview)

You were a story consultant for *Dirty Dancing* by spending the summer of 1985 telling Eleanor Bergstein your story—going through photos of the era, clothing, hair styles, and discussing your years of being a dance pro at Grossinger's from 1954 to 1986. Now we are at the twenty-fifth anniversary of *Dirty Dancing*. What would you like to say about the twenty-fifth anniversary of *Dirty Dancing*?

JACKIE: Well, what happened because of this weekend, it's even more awesome. I'm teaching at a hotel in the Catskills now called Kutsher's. We have an upcoming *Dirty Dancing* Latin weekend—all Latin dances—the end of July.

This one woman who's a guest this weekend came to me. She doesn't know who I am. And my name is just Jackie. For the classes that I'm giving, I hadn't said anything yet. I had not done any lecture yet. And she says, "You know, this brings back so many memories. You're doing a mambo class, a salsa class. Do you know how long I've been doing that? And how many times I have watched the film *Dirty Dancing*?" She said, "I watched it yesterday. In the car, I watch it every single day."

And I started to cry.

Oh.

JACKIE: I can't believe this—when we were told, "It was a nothing," so many years ago, and "Why bother? It's a piece of fluff." And that's all we heard. Everyone turning it down. It was just a sad moment—you want to walk away from it. And how many decades later—and we have a whole new audience for this. I had thirteen- and eighteen-year-olds in one of my classes, and believe it or not, this is their favorite dance, so I taught them some of the basic steps. "Oh, my goodness, from the real person who really did this." I said, "Yes." I was very excited about it.

So each thing brings back bittersweet memories. Everyone who comes up to me—as I had lived it and did the story and told the story—and that's how it continues on. I mean, they're really in disbelief. They don't believe it. I show them your book. . . . I'm going to be doing a *Dirty Dancing* weekend—what I do anyway because I'm there [Kutsher's] every weekend. I'm there all summer—probably there through October, November. . . . Then they close for a few months and re-open in March. . . . Wait 'til you see the poster. I am going to send you a miniature one. . . . It says: "*Dirty Dancing*'s Original Jackie Horner."

So what do you think, in your opinion, makes it such a cult film? It's like a cultural phenomenon. Why is it so popular after twenty-five years?

JACKIE: You know what, I don't understand it. I really don't—for many reasons. First of all, we've had four other Catskill films. Well, you had *A Walk on the Moon*, and you had the wonderful little hotel one, *Sweet Lorraine*, done at the Heiden Hotel next to the Raleigh Hotel. That was a famous little one. That was pretty much at the same time. And none of them really did anything except to be shown once or twice for their opening. You didn't see them again—or maybe you saw it a year or two later. . . . *Dirty Dancing*—the lines were around the block the first night it was open.

That's amazing, isn't it?

JACKIE: It was. They were just around the block. And to think, five years later, okay, all right. Ten years later, okay. To go this long and still see people buy the DVDs or anything they can get their hands on. And just watch it over and over and over. It's more than a classic. It's beyond that—as far as I am concerned. I think we'll be watching, twenty years from now, *Dirty Dancing*. It is going to go on forever. And I don't know what causes it. I don't know what it is.

And, you know, it has helped tremendously the dance business. It really has, and it continues to. Twenty-five years later, you still have people say, "I want to learn this," or, "I want to do that." And we have *Dancing with the Stars*, *So You Think You Can Dance*, and all these wonderful things that come on. I think basically because of that. I think that helped tremendously.

I have to wonder—obviously it wouldn't be *Dirty Dancing* without dancing in the movie, but that seems to be a big part of why it's so successful. Some of the dances that are in the movie: merengue, cha-cha, things like that—I mean those are just timeless.

JACKIE: Sue, even when I have just women that are doing line dancing, it's not just line dancing. I did the merengue line dance that we gave to Cynthia Rhodes to do in the film. And that was done at the Pines Hotel and it was recorded on video to take down to Asheville. I had done that as a dance.

I always use the line with the men all the time, and I always laugh about that: "You're the boss on the dance floor, if nowhere else."

That is just priceless.

JACKIE: I still use that. I still do it. There are so many stories that came out of that time. I was at Grossinger's teaching. It still hadn't closed in '86 yet. There was a family that had been coming up for maybe twenty, thirty years—and their brothers, and their children, and their wives. So this is the one story I thought you would like to hear, too. So one of the brothers comes over. His name is Louie, and he says to me, "You know, all these years my brother has never danced with you—never taken a lesson with you."

And I said, "Well, what's the problem?"

He said, "He has two left feet, or he just can't dance. My whole family dances. I don't understand it." He said, "Tell you what Jackie, I'm going to give you twenty dollars for every five minutes you can possibly get him on that dance floor. I'm giving the band two hundred dollars to play another twenty minutes."

Wow!

JACKIE: This is two in the morning, Sue. I go over, and I said to Arnie, "Your brother is giving me twenty dollars for every five minutes I can get you up on the dance floor, and I don't care if you just stand and sway."

Yeah, really.

JACKIE: He said, "He's going to give you that much?"

I said, "Let's get up and show them how we can keep you on the floor for awhile." So I got him up. I swear he must have been on the floor at least twenty minutes. That was like, wow.

Louie said, "I have to back it up. Here's your money."

Oh, that is really a cute story.

JACKIE: That's the way they were. They used to come into the dance studio to take lessons and they would—go back to any of the years 'cause they did it all the time—they would come in, like, cocktail hour. They'd come in and take their classes and lessons about five o'clock. And that way they could have their little cocktail party. The waiters and waitresses at the bar would bring down their drinks while they were taking their lessons. They weren't dancing and learning anything. They wanted a party—New Year's Eve every single day.

What about the famous champagne hour? What exactly was that? Is that what you were referring to?

JACKIE: Here's a little story that started me out on this—when I had met my husband [Lou Goldstein]. There were basketball games on Friday night. I mean, that's not just Grossinger's. It was every hotel. On Friday night, you couldn't dance or play music at that time. What they called the Borscht Belt, Sour Cream Sierras—they had names for all over the area for what these hotels were like. It was primarily really a Jewish clientele. And they were going along with the Shabbas thing, not having music and dancing. So they had basketball games. And that's how Lou got to the hotel and how a lot of the basketball players came up to work to play basketball on Friday night. . . .

And all of a sudden, in 1953, when I was invited up in the wintertime to do a show and when I had come up, it was one of their first times that they were doing a champagne hour. What they did, they sold the hotel on Friday at sundown for a dollar. The young man who was the stage manager of the night club, he would give the hotel management a dollar, and he owned the hotel that night, so we could have music and dancing.

So we had a champagne hour that went on at approximately 9:30. And all teachers—whether there were six in the winter or ten in the summer—would open with a number all together—a big number with all of us. Then we did individual numbers, and then we had a middle number. What we did is, each one of the dancers—let's say there were five males and five females—each took one from the audience. I took a man, and another dance teacher—the male—would take a woman, and each one would do a different dance. And then those dances at the end were graded by three judges on stage.

The judges were fabulous. In fact, one of them was my first pupil—Cliff Robertson. You had George Abbott—fabulous American theater, the Broadway theater. He created just so many wonderful shows: *Damn Yankees*, *Best Foot Forward*, *Music Is*, and

Fiorello! You name it—he did it. And then we had on stage at times: Jayne Mansfield, Linda Darnell, Shelley Winters, Mickey Hargitay [married to Jayne Mansfield]. These were the judges.

Oh my gosh!

JACKIE: The judge named five men and women, and one out of each won the big trophy, and the other four got a bottle of champagne. That was our champagne night, and they went on every single Friday night for the thirty-six years I taught at Grossinger's. It never finished. It never ended. And every judge was just bigger than the next. And of course, the ones (unfortunately) that I just mentioned have all left us. But at the end, there were still others there. There were always famous people in the audience—big shots, volunteers—but most of them were show business, most of them were dancers or actors or actresses. These were the people who came to the hotel. Lucille Ball—she was a love. I did many things with her. I ice-skated with her—who knows. Judy Garland I took shopping because she didn't want to be alone.

Oh, that's amazing.

JACKIE: This was, like, taken for granted. We were friends. It was just so wonderful. Memories are there forever in your heart and mind. I just wish everybody well that has passed on. And I know they're up there thinking about all of the good times we had.

I know you give a lot of lectures on the movie *Dirty Dancing*, and I wonder: are there certain questions or topics that the people who attend ask or bring up frequently?

JACKIE: First of all, you know (sad to say) how many have passed on in that the film. Because, "Oh, I remember Jerry Orbach." "Oh, what a sad thing, Patrick Swayze. . . ."

They always want to know about this step or that step, and what was popular then. . . . They still carry on about what they call now salsa. It's the same as mambo. There is no change.

Oh, is that the same? I didn't know that.

JACKIE: It's the same dance. All they do is dance on the count of 1, instead of the count of 2. Mambo and Latin dances, we dance on 2, 3, 4, and we hold for 1. But in salsa, they do it right on the downbeat. We dance on the offbeat. Of course, we had to teach that to Patrick because he didn't dance on the offbeat.

He didn't?

JACKIE: He was a jazz dancer and, you know, danced on the downbeat. So did Jennifer. My God, they were wonderful. I can't imagine anybody else being in those parts that would have done what they did. Yesterday this lady said to me, "It was the last scene that got me. She danced up there after 'Nobody puts Baby in the corner' and when she jumped into his arms, I just melt. I absolutely fall apart and cry every time."

You know, that kind of brings up the subject of the movie that's going to be the remake of the original classic, timeless movie. There is a lot of controversy about that. Just recently, this Kenny Ortega director thing was postponed indefinitely until at least 2014, supposedly due to casting problems.

JACKIE: You know, the one thing I don't really understand yet—because last summer, the manager of Kutsher's called me in and said, "You know, they want to do a remake here." This was the same time I was filming *The Last of the Mambo Dancers*. We still haven't finished yet. I haven't heard from them yet, but they're supposed to be back next summer to do some more work on that. Whether it is a documentary or whether it's going to be a movie, I don't know. So we've done a lot already on that. In fact, they even danced with the one who leases the hotel. And this is a nice little modern religious gentleman (Orthodox man), and he leases the hotel six, seven months a year. So they've been trying to work it out to get that finished. . . . I haven't heard if the *Dirty Dancing* thing is going to be done. Now they are doing another movie at Kutsher's. And today they were walking around with cameras.

What kind of movie?

JACKIE: It's not a dance movie. From what I heard, it's about a haunted house. . . . There's another movie being made too—not too far from here—maybe five, six miles from here. I don't know the name of it. . . .

So, switching the topic, for the people who didn't read the first book, do you have any specific stories that you told to Eleanor Bergstein that made it into the movie that you would like to share? Like, I know you talked about the watermelon.

JACKIE: I'm a professional dance teacher anyway. I was a ballet teacher, tap teacher besides. I had done all kinds of tours. I had done the *Milton Berle Show*—a few other things: Sid Caesar, Jackie Gleason, stuff like this. I didn't want to run around the country anymore. So when they offered me—after I had done a show up here—they offered me the job. Actually, my first private lesson was Cliff Robertson.

Oh!

JACKIE: And bless his heart. I was thrilled. But I taught very professionally—it was just another person. At the end of every one of his lessons—at that time, it was six half-hour lessons for thirty-five dollars—that's all. Now today, it is fifty to sixty dollars for a private lesson. It was thirty-five dollars for all six. Now at the end of every lesson, he would hand me money—a five, a twenty, a fifty, or whatever. I would put it in an envelope and take it to my bosses, Lucille and Tony [Colon]. I took it over from them—they both had passed away in the early seventies already. But anyways, I gave the six lessons. At the end of the six lessons, he said to me, "Jackie, would you put what I owe you on my bill? I'll pay it all at once at the front."

I didn't say anything. I didn't want to look stupid. I wrote out the charge slip, and I took it into my boss. I gave her that funny look. She's waving an envelope, and she said, "Sweetheart, you'll learn, these are your tips."

That is so cute.

JACKIE: What he was giving me in cash was my tip. A hundred and fifty dollars at that time—that was probably rent for the month. It was unbelievable. I couldn't understand that at all.

We had moments. What was going on was great. I finally found out how we could get involved. You see, the dance studio, the teachers were more or less considered the upper echelon. We ate in the main dining room. We danced with all the guests. We could sit with them at the table. We could go into the pool with them because the dance studio, in the summer, was upstairs. We didn't have to have keys to just get in because that's where we were. No other staff were permitted anywhere. They couldn't even walk up toward the dining room. The band had to go through the kitchen below. They had to go through the hallways. No staff could be seen at the bar. I don't care how you were dressed. You were not allowed in the inner part of the hotel.

So in order to go to their wonderful evenings—because when they would finish maybe ten o'clock, cleaning up the dining room, whatever; and then around eleven-thirty, twelve they would have their own parties and their own dances—Latin dances—or whatever they wanted to do. And we had a building on the grounds where one of our Bungalow Bunnies lived—the real one—she lived upstairs. The building was called Holiday Inn, by the way. It's on a little lake right at the entrance of the outdoor pool at Grossinger's, which was 100' x 200', a huge place. . . . And cabanas where the stars sat all day long. It was this nice little building. That's also the building where we used to have movies in there with Rocky Marciano, and Lou [Goldstein, my husband] and I would entertain some of our guests, the Yankees and everybody.

And in the summer in the evenings—and it wasn't every single night, it was two or three nights a week—they would have their parties. And they liked to dance. Every season we had a show that was written by one of the staff, and I choreographed all the dance numbers, and we presented that on Labor Day to all the guests. Meanwhile, I had a pretty good entry to the waiters and waitresses. Everybody loved the dance teachers anyways. So as a little token when the show was over, at eleven-thirty, twelve, when I finished dancing with my pupils, I went to the kitchen to the salad bar area, and I would get a watermelon. So then I would plug it with vodka. The teachers, maybe four or five of us, we would go to the Holiday Inn. We would walk out the main dining room in the back, walk up the walkway, and there was a beautiful building on a little lake—it used to be the ice-skating rink—and we would go in and I would give them the watermelon. They would all cut it up nicely, and do whatever they wanted with it. And we would dance—as long as we would do a little exhibition and dance it together, we felt like we belonged. We broke the ice that way. I must have done that for about a month. Somewhere the end of July, August, I go in one night and there's a watermelon sitting out on the counter with a note: "Jackie, it's our secret. I know you've been doing this for months. Now keep on doing it. I'll have it here. Just let me know what night you're doing it. You got the watermelon? How many more do you need?"

Oh, that is so cute. That was so nice. Wow!

JACKIE: You know, you don't forget those things. Every once in a while, a lot of those members of the staff, especially after Lou's passing [April 2, 2012]: One of them came to me, "Jackie, don't you remember me? I was—" such and such. "Don't you remember me? Remember I did this and I did that." The people are in their seventies, sixties, and eighties. I said, "Of course, I remember all of those things." How do you forget something? They're all memories. You don't forget those wonderful things. They're all great. Like the movie goes on—so do all the stories of the Catskills. Everyone has a story—there are millions. You can never stop talking about this. Everyone I talk to has their own story, and more. And it is forever. Each one.

We had one story—now Lou [he was Activities and Entertainment Director at Grossinger's where he honed his comedy shows and was famous for "Simon Says" games] was doing his show at 10:30 in the morning, every morning. The boss was Harry Grossinger at that time. Oh, he walks in the lobby, he's so frustrated. He's so upset. He's almost in tears. And I'm standing on the side getting ready because I do a side after Lou. He says, "Oh, it's shocking. It's terrible. It's awful. Oh, my God. Vandalism, I don't know what they're doing."

Lou said, "Calm down. What's the matter?"

He said, "I just went through the Eddie Cantor building. You don't know what they've done. There's no doors. And the rooms. They're laying on the floor. There's mattresses and people all over the place, and bottles. I've never seen this in all my life at the hotel. I have to own this hotel and look at this."

Lou says, "Look, sit down for a second." Now the guests were listening to this. Lou: "You have to understand, this family comes here about eight times a year. Now, I'll tell you something else. There's never a single person that's left out of the group. At the bar, when drinking there, I want you to know they spend about six thousand dollars at the bar every single night."

He goes, "Oy vey. Oh my goodness." He said, "We'll fix the doors when they leave."

Oh!

JACKIE: How much money these families spent. This is what it was. Money just flowed. One family—they're all together and they took every room in the building. They didn't care. They didn't need doors. The dance studio was in the Roosevelt building—walk out and go down the hall—that would take you to another outside building they had connected. At the top of the stairs was the barbershop.

This family would take the barber when they would go in and shave him, and put shaving cream all over the place. Then they would call people in and give them about a hundred dollars to clean it up.

Oh my gosh!

JACKIE: This was the guests we had. This was crazy. This went on and on and on. Lots of laughs, honey. Lots of laughs.

If you wouldn't mind, I know you told me before a story about Shelley Winters and practicing the lifts in the water.

JACKIE: Shelley Winters, first of all, I guess she was a friend from the moment she came to Grossinger's, from the very first time. I know I had met her in New York previously. She hadn't married Tony Franciosa yet either, at that time. She would call me, and she would say—she had a big Cadillac, a yellow Cadillac—and she would say, "I've gotta bring the car in. I'm going to drive up. I need an oil change." I said, "To take the car for an oil change—that was your reason for coming up?" She said, "No, I like the food." Bless her heart. She loved the food. She was wonderful to the guests. Not that anybody bothered—the guests never bothered anybody when they were eating. But she didn't care: You want to come over, you want to talk, and you want to sit down—that was fine with Shelley.

So we're sitting at the table one night. All these people are coming around and they're talking to her. And she says to me, "You know, Jackie, I didn't want to say anything, but did you notice that I was watching the dance rehearsal this afternoon?"

I said, "Sure."

She said, "Well, I didn't kind of like what I saw."

"What's the matter?"

She said—do you know, at that time, you know we work out? I mean there were ballerina lifts, maybe, or they're knee lifts. . . . She said, "The men wore suits. They wore tuxedos. And they had cuf-flinks. You know, all you have to do is get caught on that, and you're up in the air and you're doing that and how easy it is to fall on that wooden floor—how you could hurt yourself doing all those lifts?"

"You know, I never thought about it because we do it so automatically. Sure, I've tripped on occasion. Sure, I did a back bend too far. I never really fell when doing a lift."

She said, "You know something. Take my advice. Go down to the lake this Sunday. I'm going to be down there. You know I go down there every Sunday with my books. I sit at the chaise lounge by the lake. Practice your lifts in the lake."

And that was in the afternoon. So I said, "You know, it's not a bad idea." So I got a hold of all the teachers. We were off on Sunday—unless you wanted to teach (you could teach on your own if you wanted to—no one forced you). You were off Sunday. So what we did, we went down to the lake—six or seven of us. And we worked on our lifts in that water in the lake. So when we fell, it was wonderful. That was added to the movie.

That is so amazing.

JACKIE: All of these little things were so real. So every time something happened, I wrote it down.

One night, I'm standing in the nightclub with Eddie Fisher's manager. Now, when I look back at Grossinger's, my husband, Lou Goldstein, was Eddie Fisher's roommate. And Debbie Reynolds came up to me and she sat with me and we always were together and we watched him and that's how she sort of got involved. She had nothing to do with it.

Louie would say, you know, two things—he said, "You know when Eddie Fisher has someone in his room, he put a towel on the door. He put the towel on the door so I knew not to go in there."

I said, "Lou, why don't you put the towel on the door some night, so you can get some sleep."

Lou, "You know, I never thought of it. So one night I put the towel on the door and Eddie couldn't believe I would have a girl in the room."

He said, "Lou would have a girl in the room!"

"Honey, you know he had five girlfriends. He had five that he proposed to."

One night I'm standing with Milton Blackstone (that's Eddie Fisher's manager), and Milton is saying to me—now I'm in a small club and the Latin band was playing and it's the most beautiful dance and my couples are all practicing. It's three in the morning already. Milton comes over and said, "It is time for my dance lesson."

I said, "It's too late. My pupils I'm watching. I have to get to bed. I get up at nine in the morning."

He said, "All right, but I have to tell you something. They're dancing too close."

"What are you talking about, Milton? They're doing a tango. They dance close."

He says, "No, this hotel is a chic hotel. This is a beautiful hotel—classy. They're dancing dirty."

I said, "Really." And I wrote it down. This is what I wrote with Shelley—this is what I wrote with him—bits and pieces all those years I was around. It sounded great to me. Like today, I keep a diary of every single day of my life 'cause I don't know what I may do next. So I can't tell. I want to know those little bits and pieces. You know, I don't want them to slip away—the dates and times of those things that happened. These are the things that happened.

Wow, that's just so amazing!

JACKIE: It's all real. Nothing could be better than real. When someone looked at the movie, they said, "You know, it's real. It happened. It's truth. You can't make up these things."

EXCERPT FROM JACKIE HORNER'S BIOGRAPHICAL SKETCH[1]*

Jackie Horner was born in a small town in southern Ohio to parents who were both active in musical endeavors. While she was engaged in modeling at age four, she, and her parents became increasingly aware of her love for music accentuated by the beat of her dancing feet. They knew that her future would be transcended beyond the sphere of the posing little Miss Horner.

Hence, the dance was soon to capture Jackie's total interest. She was to study beyond the norm under such celebrated dance masters as Grace Bedell, Deborah Hoffman, Henry Le Tang, Jose Limon, and Jack Stanley in New York; and Carol Linn of the Peabody Conservatory of Music in Baltimore. . . .

Ms. Horner has danced throughout the United States, Canada, Mexico and South America in night clubs, theaters, and television's top variety shows. . . . At present, she teaches dance here in the Catskills, colleges, regional theaters, and choreographs musical theater productions as well as appearing in some. . . . The Catskills are her magical mountains where her happiest moments have been spent teaching the stars of Hollywood, television and all the guests who come on vacations these many years.

Note: The sketch also states that Ms. Horner was a Rockette and a member of the June Taylor dance company.

***Special thanks to Jackie Horner for permission to use this excerpt from her biographical sketch.**

Courtesy of Jackie Horner.

Champagne Hour at Grossinger's in the summer of 1955: Steve Schwartz with Lucille Colon, Jackie Horner with Tony Colon, and another couple. (Steve Schwartz is said to be one of the people whom Johnny Castle is based on.)

Courtesy of Jackie Horner.

Jackie Horner at Grossinger's in 1957.

Courtesy of Jackie Horner.

Jackie Horner and Steve Schwartz dancing at Grossinger's in 1955.

Courtesy of Jackie Horner.

Jackie Horner (fourth back on the right), Steve Schwartz (second back on the left) and other teachers at Grossinger's in 1955.

Courtesy of Jackie Horner.

Jackie Horner with Saul Fagen doing a mambo exhibition on Jackie's birthday at Grossinger's on July 9, 1964.

Courtesy of Jackie Horner.

Franc Peri, Jackie Horner, and Lou Perez (on flute) at Grossinger's.

Courtesty of Steve Schwartz.

Steve Schwartz and Nadine Leach in Miami Beach in 1956.
This is the poster for the Mambo Jamboree that he ran at the De Lido Hotel.
Steve Schwartz, also known by his professional name, Steve Sands,
was the dance partner of Jackie Horner at Grossinger's in the '50s.
Per Jackie Horner, "He's the Johnny (Patrick Swayze)."

The famous Mountain Lake gazebo where many key scenes were filmed—like where Baby and her father had their heart-to-heart talk and Baby had her foot stepped on by a male guest during a dance class.

CHAPTER EIGHT

JIM MYERS

EXECUTIVE CHEF AT MOUNTAIN LAKE, 1980–1986

KAREN MYERS

DINING ROOM MANAGER AT MOUNTAIN LAKE, 1980–1986

Lynchburg, Virginia
August 17, 2012 (telephone interview)

What were your positions during the *Dirty Dancing* 1986 filming at Mountain Lake?

JIM: I was the Executive Chef for the hotel.

Wow. How long had you been there? When did you start?

JIM: We came in 1980, and we left, actually, the day after *Dirty Dancing* wrapped—September 20, 1986.

Really. Wow. Have you been back there since?

KAREN: Many times.

JIM: Oh, sure. We actually won a free weekend up there in a raffle.

That's excellent.

KAREN: We have lots of friends still from that area, having been there that long.

What can you tell me about the famous scene that was filmed in the kitchen in which Penny crouches in the corner and Johnny comes to rescue her?

JIM: Well, it was a bit problematic for me because I had a really tacit agreement with the guys on the crew that they would be finished by four o'clock in the morning because that's when I had to go in and start prepping breakfast while making biscuits. Of course, they were not done.

Uh-oh.

JIM: Well, it's always that way, I think. So I had to start my prep in the corner in the dark. That was a bothersome thing. Of course, it was interesting to watch them do everything. The kitchen was fairly large, but they were in a very cramped spot next to the—I think it was the dairy refrigerator—stuck in the corner there. They didn't have a lot of room to move. Of course, it reduced the flexibility of the camera angles. They were really nice about it and apologizing, you know, and all. So I just tried to be nice back, but they finally got out in time for me to get breakfast up for the regular guests.

They must have had to reshoot several times or something.

JIM: They shot it all night long from as many different angles as they could. They did a lot of takes, a lot of takes on each little dialogue.

I visited Mountain Lake, and of course I had my picture taken there by Buzz Scanland [then the General Manager at Mountain Lake, who had been doing marketing during filming]. I couldn't pass that one up. I look horrible in the picture, but I guess the scene looks okay. I think Mike Porterfield [the current Executive Chef at Mountain Lake, who was Lead Line Cook during filming] had told me, when I spoke to him a

couple of years ago, that's one of the most photographed areas over there at Mountain Lake. Who in the cast or the crew did you have contact with, and what type of contact?

JIM: The first one that I got to know was Jerry Orbach, and he was just a real gentleman. We just had a couple of decent conversations. We didn't have any social time with each other. Then Jennifer—we met Jennifer a couple of times and she was just a sweetie-pie. She was just pleasant. She had a nice attitude. She wasn't at all arrogant. She was, like, "homesey"—real people.

She was seeing Matthew Broderick then, and he came up to visit with her. He was sitting on the bench out in front of our room—what had been our room on Lakeview, and he and I sat and chatted.

KAREN: Matthew was very kind. He took some of the staff's kids out fishing while Jennifer was filming. They had a great time. Everybody just thought a lot of him.

JIM: And Patrick—I was extremely busy the whole time they were there. I only shook hands with Patrick, and he was a very nice fellow. He had a much better temperament than a lot of the others. Actually, I think Patrick and Jennifer and . . .

KAREN: Jerry.

JIM: Jerry Orbach and Paula Trueman, they were just, like, the nicest of the nice. I think most of the actors were pretty nice and, you know, straightforward people. A lot of the directing assistants were hard to deal with, and some of the dancers were. Gay and Giles county in 1985 or '86—they didn't interface very well. So there was a lot of talk among the staff about some of the guests.

Just jumping back a second, you mentioned Paula Trueman, I think, Jim—is she the gal that played the elderly lady that was purse snatching?

JIM: Paula Trueman. Yeah, they were the sneak thieves—her and her husband in the movie. I saw her later in *Outlaw Josey Wales*. . . . She was really cute, very energetic.

KAREN: Like Jim said—he was cooking all the time because we had to rotate between the time he was cooking for the principals, cast, and crew and the time he was cooking for the regular guests. He was doing double duty and so was I, in the dining room with double duty. So we were just busy all the time.

It was part of my job as Dining Room Manager to make sure that principals were not harassed by staff or by guests. I remember this one time, one of the regular guests came up to me. He had asked for an autograph for I can't remember who—his daughter, his mother, his wife, I don't know. I somehow decided that I would do this for him. So when Mr. Swayze came through the dining room, I asked him, "Would you mind doing me a really big favor? I really hate to ask this, but could you please sign an autograph for one of the guests?" And he said, "Sure. Sure. No problem. What's her name?" And I had not asked the gentleman who this was for. Patrick paused for a minute, and he wrote, "To a lovely lady," and signed it, which I thought was just very, very sweet.

Yeah. That's a cute story. So Jim, what was it like to cook for the *Dirty Dancing* cast and crew? Did they have special requests?

JIM: Well, no. You know actors and dancers are pretty often weird about their diet. We did try to do a few more vegetarian and lighter fare. They had craft services on the property too. They took care of coffee, doughnuts, and snacks and stuff like that. Generally, I put up the same menu for them as I did for the regular guests. We didn't have a ton of regular guests, but we had a bridge tournament and long-term guests that we couldn't just turn out. I think that might have been a point in the contract. I think they wanted the whole place, but we had to fight them on that to keep our regular guests and the long-term bookings.

KAREN: When the bridge tournament came, it was part of the negotiation. The movie people knew they had to vacate the hotel because we were booked solid for the bridge tournament.

JIM: Like Karen said, the regular guests ate [at] one time and the principals ate an hour later. I had to put the same menu up twice—three times a day.

Wow.

JIM: There were not a lot of good restaurants around. We were seven miles from anywhere there, and a lot of them didn't have cars and stuff. They were pretty much prisoners there. I tried to do as well for them as I could. We were real busy, but fortunately I had a really good staff there then, too, and they were all real dependable.

So how many people were you cooking for from the cast and crew?

JIM: With the principals, director, designer—probably twenty-five or thirty of them I guess. Occasionally, they would bring extras in, but not as a rule.

KAREN: Wives would visit and different things like that.

Did you ever see Patrick Swayze's wife there?

KAREN: I think she did come up. I'm not positive about that, but I do think I remember somebody pointing her out.

What about the water lift scene? I'm pretty sure it was filmed at Mountain Lake, but you hear it was filmed at the other location.

KAREN: No, it was filmed at Mountain Lake.

Yeah.

KAREN: It was cold water. That water was cold.

How cold?

KAREN: I don't know how cold, but it was cold. I do remember that they had all these makeup tables and different kinds of tables set up on the beach, and as long as the guests did not interfere or come within a certain boundary, they were certainly welcome to watch, but they got kind of bored, I remember, because, as you probably know, with movie-making: it's stop-start, start-again, retake, retake, retake, retake, lots of waiting, waiting, waiting, waiting. The guests were real excited at first, and then they're like, this is boring.

That must have been really hard to go in that cold water for Jennifer and Patrick.

JIM: Yeah. The scene with the big tree over that stream—that was done at the other location. That was another water scene.

There was a big tree over the stream?

JIM: They're playing around on the small little tree and there's water under it as I recall.

KAREN: The log . . .

Balancing on the log. And that's the scene they used to make a statue of Patrick for the Madame Tussauds [Wax Museum] Hollywood.

KAREN: Right, that was the other location. . . . They might have reshot the water lift scene there [Lake Lure], but I know that they shot the scene at Mountain Lake.

So why do you think *Dirty Dancing* is still so popular?

JIM: I think it was very fortunate, timing-wise. They were at the right place, at the right time, with a really feel-good coming-of-age movie. It's all so very young, and so much of it is upbeat. Even the bad stuff is not as horrible as some of the things you see now. Timing and the cast. The cast was just remarkable.

KAREN: Certainly, the music, and certainly, the dancing—especially Patrick, Cynthia, and Jennifer.

JIM: It was all very contemporary, too—just what was hot. I think it had a lot of things going for it. The script and the result actually had a lot more going for it than Vestron did. Anyway, the product was just right, you know, and it's something you can watch over and over again.

Do you watch it a lot?

JIM: We've watched it probably ten or fifteen times, I guess.

KAREN: The first time we saw it in the theater, we didn't know what to expect. We had to, of course, go see it. It was really fun to go, "Okay, that's Mountain Lake. That's North Carolina. That's Mountain Lake. That's North Carolina." They turn a corner, and they see Mountain Lake on approaching the corner, and they see North Carolina when they went around the corner. That was kind of fun to see.

What was the name of the theater where you saw it? Was it the Lyric or something?

KAREN: No, we just saw it locally.

Oh, gotcha. Okay.

JIM: We were gone. It didn't come out for almost a year after we had left.

KAREN: We had moved away.

That's right. You said that before. Do you have a favorite scene or actor/actress in the movie?

JIM: My favorite scene is the one on the gazebo with Jerry Orbach and Jennifer Grey. The pond was full, and the gazebo was new and immaculate and really pretty. Our daughter was christened on that gazebo. We really like that part.

Oh! Is that where they have the heart-to-heart talk?

JIM: Yeah. He's in the rocking chair.

KAREN: I also like, of course, the dancing. Patrick is such a graceful dancer. I like the sister's talent act. That was a crack-up.

JIM: That was funny.

KAREN: I like the lover-boy scene where they're on the floor and they're, like, miming. I thought that was kind of a fun scene.

Supposedly, they improvised on that one. I think.

KAREN: Really.

Yeah.

KAREN: You certainly see the connection between Patrick and Jennifer.

You know you hear all those rumors they didn't get along at all on the set, and blah, blah, blah, blah, blah.

KAREN: But it did not come across on the screen. On the screen, they really connected.

I think that's a big part of the success too. Now we get into the remake of *Dirty Dancing*. Kenny Ortega is the director. What do you guys think about that?

JIM: I think it's really hard for sequels to equal, you know, the original. Although he was there for that, I mean, he didn't have all of the responsibilities of a director. I don't know. I just sort of hold my breath and wait and see.

KAREN: I mean, as much as we have feelings about the movie, I kind of feel like, why not? I think it would be interesting to see the changes, but I think he certainly would have a challenge in recapturing the feeling that the movie generated.

What else do you want to say about your experience there when they were filming at Mountain Lake for *Dirty Dancing*?

JIM: I remember when they first came in, there was just confusion all over the place. Then, when they were doing the big scenes with all of the show cars, that was just really wonderful to watch. I'm an old-car buff. That was a hoot. The inside jokes. You know, I don't remember any specifics, but we had lots of comments about just about everybody.

KAREN: As I am sure they had about us.

JIM: It was a very exciting time, certainly, but it was also at the end of my tenure, and I was itching to get out because we'd just gotten our job in Miami. We were very much looking forward to that. I guess in some ways, it prepped me a little bit for what I was going to be going through when I would be working for Don Johnson.

Don Johnson?

JIM: We left there to be Don Johnson's personal chef and hostess.

Wow. Anything you want to say about that experience?

KAREN: They flew us down in the midst of the filming and interviewed and hired us prior to finishing up there.

So what was it like working for Don Johnson?

JIM: Oh, he was just a really nice guy at home. He might have been a beast on the set, but at home he was mannerly and well behaved. Trouble was, he wasn't eating red meat. He was on these diets that made me crazy because I'm a roast cook, you know. So I had to deal with that. We met just so many people.

KAREN: Lovely people.

JIM: At his house there, he had a screening room, and he would run first-run movies there before they even opened to the public. We had a professional popcorn popper, and he liked to have Vanilla Swiss Almond Häagen-Dazs for dessert.

Wow.

JIM: He had 35mm projectors in there, and a great big screen, and we would do theme dinners for between thirty and a hundred people every weekend because he just didn't like to go out.

KAREN: Because it was hard for him without being, you know—the fans would make it sometimes hard for him to have quiet time.

Wow. I haven't heard too much about him lately.

JIM: Well, there isn't too much going on that we know about. I know he won his suit. He sued some studio over *Nash Bridges* . . . We were there in the third season of *Miami Vice*, and it was really the hottest thing going.

I loved that show.

JIM: Oh yeah. And all of them came to Don's place one time or another while we were there, except Philip Michael. It was a lot of fun. . . .

KAREN: I did want to say one other thing about the movie. The manager at the time was J.C. Mac Millan. His last name was Mac Millan—everyone called him Mac. When they first came in for the negotiation, there was some trepidation about the words *Dirty Dancing*, which was the working title at that time. They changed the working title to *Dancing* just to keep everybody kind of—you don't know what it means, *Dirty Dancing*—-until you've seen the movie. . . . I have a pretty good feeling that when they walked out of the negotiation, the movie people felt like they had gotten a great deal, and Mac and the hotel felt like they had gotten a great deal.

That's good.

KAREN: Yeah. It started off on a really positive, and I think it ended on a positive note. But it really started very well. They both felt like they had gotten a good deal.

JIM: They still get crowds for their *Dirty Dancing* weekend things, too.

That's good. Unfortunately, I was there, like January 6th, and it was, like, twenty below zero or something. Oh well. Timing is everything—right? In a way, it was good. I was about the only one there. Buzz just sat me down there in the room with a big book of archives. I got a lot of pictures.

Is there anything else that comes to mind about the movie?

JIM: It was just a really exciting time for everybody. It was really an unusual event for the people who lived on the mountain. And that was just so amusing time after time: "Do you know what he did?"

Oh, wow. I mean it sounds like it's something you'll never forget.

JIM: Oh, no.

KAREN: Oh, absolutely. I will not forget it.

I wish I had been there.

Courtesy of Sue Tabashnik. Photo by Buzz Scanland.

Here I am in this famous kitchen where Penny (Cynthia Rhodes) crouched down crying, and soon Johnny (Patrick Swayze) arrived to rescue her.

Credit: Sue Tabashnik.

The Mountain Lake dining room where many key scenes were filmed.

Courtesy of Mountain Lake Hotel.

The Houseman family's table in the dining room at "Kellerman's."

Credit: DJ Rick Pruett.

The Mountain Lake Patrick Swayze Memorial Stone, which was dedicated in November 2009.

Credit: Sue Tabashnik.

"Buzz" Scanland, general manager at Mountain Lake Hotel in 2009, was a very gracious host to me during my visit there.

Credit: Sue Tabashnik.

The front of Mountain Lake Hotel, taken by me during my January 2009 visit.

Credit: Sue Tabashnik.

Mountain Lake Hotel cottages.

Credit: Sue Tabashnik.

The Mountain Lake gazebo with the Houseman Cottage in the background.

Mike Porterfield, Executive Chef at Mountain Lake Hotel, is standing in front of the hotel. He gave Patrick Swayze a ride on his motorcycle down the mountain when Dirty Dancing *was filming there, and was one of the people who hung out with Patrick Swayze, Miranda Garrison, and others in the evenings.*

Courtesy of Mountain Lake Hotel (now Mountain Lake Lodge).

The beautiful Mountain Lake Hotel.

Courtesy of Betty Rollins.

Jack and Betty Rollins and Tom and Patt Rocks—all extras at the Lake Lure set, go to the movie theater to see their work in Dirty Dancing.

CHAPTER NINE

TOM & PATT ROCKS

EXTRAS, *DIRTY DANCING*, LAKE LURE FILM LOCATION
Spartanburg, South Carolina
April 22, 2012 (telephone interview)

How did you hear about the *Dirty Dancing* movie call for extras? How did you get involved?

TOM: Patt and I met on the dance floor, and we've been dancing all our lives. And so we're known around Spartanburg with some of our friends that, if somebody is looking for dancers, you know we would certainly be interested. We had not originally heard the advertising that was going on. There was an ad in the paper looking for bodies to participate as extras and also advertised on the radio. We had originally not heard that, and some of our friends told us that they were hearing these ads looking for people. Then, after we were sort of sensitized to that, we went up to Hendersonville (which is in the Lake Lure vicinity) for an audition, and that's how we initially made contact and got involved.

Who did the auditions?

TOM: Well, there was a young lady. . . . Patt, do you remember her name? That might come to us, but there was a young lady that had some responsibility. She was with the film. She was probably, I'm guessing, twenty-five years old.

PATT: I think they were just some production assistants, and they were only looking for extras, just, you know, to fill in. They weren't looking for any stars. They just wanted to have some people to fill in for the scenes when they were sitting around or when they were dancing or whatever. So I think most of these were just PAs. Kenny [Ortega] was not involved in the audition for these roles, shall we say.

TOM: These folks were looking for warm bodies to fill the auditorium during some dance scenes and the final scene and so forth.

So you signed up right away?

PATT: Well, originally we told them no because they said, if you signed up, you had to sign up for at least a week or so. We both had jobs. So we said we really needed to think about it. We just didn't have time to be up there for a week or so, so we weren't sure we could give them all of the days they needed. We were kind of cool about it at first, but we said, you know, let's think about it. They actually had music and you could dance . . . I guess they were observing dances . . .They approached us and said, "We understand that you may not do the whole seven or eight days or whatever it may take, but we would really like for you to do this. Would you give us at least three days?" And, of course, our egos shot up about 100 percent. We said, "Yeah, we think we can do that." That was pretty exciting that they wanted us. So that's how we actually got connected and said we are committed to doing at least three days of shooting for the film.

Nobody knew anything about the film, Sue. They would not even tell us the title. One of the cast members told me the title. Everyone kept asking, but none of us knew what kind of film, you know, if it's just about dancing. We didn't know the plot. We didn't know the title.

Did you know that Patrick and Jennifer were going to be in it?

PATT: Tom, we probably knew that, didn't we?

TOM: I don't know if we knew that before we went up. We might have. We just knew they were going to be making a movie about dancing. Once we were up there, when people were saying, "What is the name going to be?" I think they were concerned about telling people in the Bible Belt that it was going to be *Dirty Dancing*. They said, "Oh, we've been thinking about calling it 'We Had the Time of Our Life,'" or something like that. Certainly, once we got up there, we knew that Patrick and Jennifer and Cynthia were going to be in it. We knew Patrick earlier through his work with *North and South*, *Red Dawn*, and that sort of thing. Jennifer was in *Red Dawn* as well. I don't know that I remember knowing who was going to be in it before we went up there or that that was part of our attraction.

How much did you get paid?

PATT: Thirty dollars a day.

TOM: And a brown bag lunch.

PATT: And some days we didn't get paid. The film was in deep financial trouble. It almost got turned over to the bonding company. The producer that we met, and I talked to, and had conversation . . .

TOM: Gottlieb.

PATT: Linda Gottlieb was going to New York every day trying to get money. We eventually would get paid, but not necessarily every day. But I will tell you, I would have paid them to have had the experience. I mean, the money was not important. It was just making a memory, having fun.

TOM: Seeing how movies are made.

PATT: They would give us meals for whatever meal times we were there. If we got released early, we didn't have dinner. There was food. We were in an open tent. It was cold. It was raining. There was nothing glamorous about it. And then if you stayed over, that was your expense—your responsibility. So meals and thirty dollars a day, and it was worth every minute that we gave to it. At some point—and I don't know why they liked us, I really don't—but they came to us and said, "We have this scene and we would like for you to be in it, but if you are, you'll have to commit to the rest of the shooting time." And at that point, we were hooked, and I said, "Wild horses won't get me out of this thing." So we committed to the full shooting time.

TOM: So we wound up being there seven or eight days after all, but we enjoyed it. But just going into it, we weren't sure if we wanted to commit that much time away from the job—vacation time. But we did, and it was great.

What scenes were you in?

TOM: There are basically two scenes. About ten minutes into the movie when Jennifer goes in—when Baby goes in—and dances with the nerdy grandson. We're placed right next to them—depending on which angle the camera is looking. I'm in a white dinner jacket and Patt is in a yellow sleeveless cocktail dress. So we can be seen in that opening scene. That's when Patrick and Cynthia show out, and—what's his name? The hotel . . .

PATT: Jack Weston.

TOM: Jack Weston comes in and tells them to cut it out—that they should be dancing with the guests and not showing out. So that scene there, we show up several times, depending on which way the camera is looking. We were placed next to Jennifer because we dance comfortably. We weren't trying to compete with anybody. We were the kind of people that—our dancing was the kind of just informal dancing that they wanted to have as hotel guests. That's the way we dance normally. And then in the final scene, I guess at the amateur competition on stage that eventually led to Patrick coming in and all that business, we show up several times there.

There's a scene I don't know (I assume you have looked at the movie a number of times)—there is a scene that shows the Bungalow Bunny sitting very bored and so forth, and the empty chair on her right, and her husband's off doing something else, and the camera pans past her and then on down the line. Patt was sitting right next to her, so she fills up the screen for a few moments.

PATT: A nanosecond.

TOM: But literally fills up the screen.

PATT: And then it goes to the end of the row, and you can see Tom, and he's right next to Baby's parents when Patrick comes in and says the great line, "Nobody puts Baby in a corner."

Oh my gosh!

PATT: And remember the extras. . . . We worked every day. A lot of the extras did not. We were called in every day for a few moments. . . .

TOM: We were all hanging out in an open-air tent and it was rainy and cold. And then the ballroom was about fifty or a hundred yards away. We had, you know, tennis shoes on. . . .

PATT: Boots.

TOM: Yeah, [we] had on boots and tennis shoes walking through the mud to get to the set, which was this sort of a gymnasium thing that had been converted into a ballroom. And once we got into the building, then we would change into dress shoes, et cetera, and roll our pants down and so forth. At any rate, that was—in other words, we didn't hang out in the tent. Every day we got to go to the set. A number did, but a number just hung out in the tent all the time.

How many extras were there?

PATT: I am thinking maybe a couple hundred—the number you see in the final scene, and that also included the *Dirty Dancing* kids—both professionally and locally. They had about nine professional *Dirty Dancing* kids, and then they went to different studios and got young people (teenagers—sixteen, seventeen, eighteen) to be the extra *Dirty Dancing* kids that you saw when they would go up into the cabin and do their dancing—when she said, "I carried a watermelon." I guess from the final scene, Tom, wouldn't you say a couple hundred?

TOM: I'd say two to three hundred—something in that order. It could have been one-hundred-fifty—could have been two-hundred-fifty. At the same time, what I remember hearing was that there would be just a lot of people, just kind of hanging around. I don't think they really turned away anybody. And they would have people get discouraged with this hurry up and waiting, and not getting called on and so forth, and so they would leave.

Then they would bring in more people. . . . It was kind of tough for folks that just hung around and didn't come to the set, et cetera.

PATT: A couple of times, when they heard grumblings and so forth, they'd say, "Okay, we need to do a crowd scene." They would pull us in (and that might be the scene that they used at the end), but if people started really getting "I don't know why I am sitting around and not doing anything." It would be in the dark of night, actually, is when they wanted us to show up.

TOM: Six o'clock for costumes and makeup and all that sort of thing.

PATT: If you hadn't done anything by three or four o'clock, you could be kind of "What am I doing here? It's cold. I don't have anything to do."

I mean, you would read or something like that. Then they'd say, "Let's do a crowd scene," and they would usher everybody in so they wouldn't get too annoyed or impatient. Even if it was just a few minutes, we did get on the set every day.

You know, there was a lot of tragedy after that movie.

What do you mean?

PATT: Emile died. One of the professional dancers was murdered in New York. Robbie [played by Max Cantor] committed suicide. Of course, eventually Patrick—of course, but I mean that was not too long—within a couple of years or so I think. It didn't happen all in a row.

Emile?

PATT: Emile [Ardolino], the director, and he was a prince of a guy. But the most beloved person connected with the movie on the set every day was Kenny Ortega. Everybody adored Kenny. I can say this now because Robbie is gone: He and Robbie did not get along. But Robbie was Robbie, on and off screen.

Wasn't it a heroin overdose that Robbie died from?

PATT: Yeah, some kind of, I don't know if I ever knew the details. It wasn't stretching for Robbie to do his part. And yet, he was a friend to me, and he is actually the one who told me, he said, "Look, they're telling these people they do not know what the name of the movie is going to be. The name of the title is going to be *Dirty Dancing*." Tom and I got to be friends with some of the cast members. I eventually had about an hour interview with Ellen . . .

TOM: The screenwriter.

Eleanor Bergstein?

PATT: Yes. At the time, I was doing a local cable television show.

TOM: Patt produced and moderated local-origination shows for about twenty-five years.

Wonderful.

PATT: And so I got a wonderful interview with Eleanor. And then

I also got some alone time with Patrick, just by accident, and had about a twenty-minute conversation with him, actually, standing at a bar having a drink.

What was Patrick like?

PATT: I thought Patrick was very nice. He came out one day. Everyone wanted to take photographs and things like that. He was very nice to the extras. His wife had just left when all the extras came in. Of course, we all know he adored his wife. He kept a couple of dogs there. They would go back to the Lake Lure Inn, where most of the principals were staying.

And one night we got off. . . . It was one of those times when we said, "Let's not go back home. Let's just stay up here for the evening and spend the night." We were at the Lake Lure Inn, and everyone was just kind of sitting around having a drink or whatever. Patrick came in.

TOM: Let me back up. We would come back to Spartanburg, which was an hour, hour and a half from Lake Lure, and we'd come back if we got off early enough, like six or seven in the evening. But if we did not get cut loose until about nine-thirty or ten, we would stay over at a motel, just around the corner from the Lake Lure Inn. This was a night that we were late and we decided to stay over. We had changed clothes out of our tuxedos and cocktail dresses into just jogging suits, you know, tennis shoes, that sort of thing. We went up to see if there was any action going on at the lounge within the Lake Lure Inn. It really was just about empty, except Honi Coles was at the bar, and so we went up and started talking to him.

PATT: And he was a delight, by the way. I adored him. He was just wonderful.

TOM: So it was just the three of us, and after ten or fifteen minutes or so, I said, "Honi, I need to go back to the motel and get some sleep . . ." and he said, "Man, you better not leave your wife alone with me." I said, "Honi, I trust you. I have to go get some sleep." And then Patt said, "You know, as long as there is anyone to talk to here, you can't carry me away." I left. Patt and Honi are talking and about five minutes later, Patrick came in, and Honi said, "Patrick, come over here. I'd like to introduce you to somebody." Patt's there in her jogging suit, and Patrick came in and said, "I know who this lady is. She's the lady in the yellow dress."

PATT: AHHH! You know, my head about burst at that point because there were just all these people around on the set, and how would he know who I was? So, you know, I was about to lose it right there. But at some point, we both got up, just to get a drink at the bar. We were talking about, you know, "How did you enjoy, of course, your visit or shooting in Charleston?" I had the South Carolina connection, and he was talking about that, and he just really opened up, and he said, "I wanted people to know that I could act before I did any singing or dancing."

Are you talking about *North and South*?

PATT: Yes. It was filmed in Charleston. We talked about restaurants in Charleston and just general chitchat. And then we got around to talking about the movie *Dirty Dancing* a little bit, and he said, "This movie is going to make me a star." And I wanted to put my arms around him and say, "Oh, you poor baby, don't count on it." Because, you know, we only saw pieces of it. And I thought, surely—I told Tom—"We'll never see this movie on the screen." I really believed that, because they were in trouble and of course we were only seeing bits and pieces. We didn't know the story. Nothing made sense. It would be like if you were looking at a movie and only saw a few minutes, and then didn't see any more, and then saw another minute or two, and that was it. I didn't feel like we were in the midst of something that was going to become a cult film. But I didn't say anything. But he did tell me that—he said, "This will make me a star." He knew.

And he said, "And all these people around, you know, the extras," he said, "Oh, they're going to see . . ." (I won't use his words.) "It is making a movie." I said, "No, Patrick. I'm in television and I am fascinated by what's going on. I think you are wrong on that. I think all the extras, when they get to be on the set, they are fascinated by the process."

But he did say that. He did tell me—he said, "This will make me a star." He was right. He knew.

We were close to Jennifer during that first scene. She was not a dancer. She had to work hard when she danced. Even though her father was a dancer, she was not. The dancer was Cynthia, and she was as sweet as she could be. She would come over to us and say, "What's going on in the extra tent?" And we started giving everybody Hollywood names. Like, we said, "Well, Elizabeth Taylor over there is doing this," and so and so. And she just loved that.

TOM: There was a woman in a red dress that, I think, during the amateur competition, she did an Elizabeth Taylor look-alike thing. And every time we'd break for lunch or something and everybody scatters, and then they come back, and the PAs . . . are checking to make sure everybody still looks the same and are in the same place. We were trying to get everybody working back in the same place, so the scene can resume. And somebody said, "Well, where were you standing?" She said, "I was standing right in front of the lady in the red dress." And at that point, Kenny Ortega spoke up and said, "I didn't think the lady in the red dress let anybody stand in front of her."

PATT: They were really very approachable and very nice. But those moments with Patrick were very special for me—just to, you know, talk and have a conversation.

TOM: I'll share another special moment for Patt. You know that Miranda was the assistant choreographer, right? The Bungalow Bunny? Typically, if Kenny needed to do something—to demonstrate something or whatever—he would have Miranda get up with him to do it. But on this particular occasion, and this is the scene where Patrick and Jennifer—when he takes her up on the stage . . .

PATT: It was for the final scene.

TOM: For the final scene. There are shots of the audience looking up at the two of them on the stage and following the action on the stage, but of course Patrick and Jennifer are not up there dancing through on the stage when the camera is all set up to take these shots of the audience, because each one of these shots takes a long time—the lighting and the sound, and, you know, all that sort of thing. So Patrick and Jennifer are not up there. That would be Kenny up there dancing the part, and he would typically get Miranda up there. But on this particular occasion when they were going to film the audience, Kenny called for Miranda, and she had gone someplace and wasn't available. So he grabbed Patt and took her up on the stage. They danced the routine that Patrick and Jennifer danced, so that the camera cuts to Patrick and Jennifer, and then it cuts to the audience, and the audience is looking lovingly at Patrick and Jennifer, but what they are really looking at is Kenny and Patt dancing the routine.

That's a nice moment to know that the audience was looking at them and not really looking at Patrick and Jennifer.

So you dance in the final number?

PATT: We are not in the film. When they cut to the *Dirty Dancing* kids—who are cheering Patrick and Jennifer doing that last dance before he jumps off the stage and she runs and he catches her—they have to have something to focus on. And they don't use the stars, if the stars are not on camera. If the camera is on the audience, it doesn't matter who is on the stage. And so Kenny and I danced so that they would have someone to focus on. Of course, when the cameras cut back to the stage, of course it was Jennifer and Patrick.

Jennifer was not an experienced dancer like Cynthia. Cynthia was just, you know, amazing, as was Patrick. Of course, everybody—their hearts went pitty-pat over Patrick, except for me. I had a chance to talk to him. He's a nice guy. I admire him. But when he danced, I couldn't catch my breath. I really couldn't. He was just a fabulous dancer.

But Jennifer was a little bit inexperienced, and she kept practicing and practicing. One day, she was walking away and her head was down, and we were right behind her. We said, "Jennifer, you are really doing a great job." And she said, "Do you really think so? Am I looking okay?" It was such a small environment. We weren't on a big studio lot. There was probably more proximity to the stars than you would normally have. She seemed to appreciate our encouragement and telling her she was doing a good job. She had to work so hard at it.

There were rumors that sometimes Jennifer and Patrick did not get along on the set. Did you notice anything like that?

PATT: No, we didn't see any of that. We heard that was more from *Red Dawn*—that they had not on *Red Dawn*. Emile, I guess, and Linda and Eleanor, felt like they would be right for *Dirty Dancing*. It wasn't obvious to me, but again, unless we were on the set, we didn't see what was going on.

TOM: I never got any hint of any kind of a problem.

PATT: Robbie was the only one that I ever heard that there were issues with, and that was with Kenny. And I don't know the background. And Kenny loved everybody, and everybody loved Kenny. But I didn't see any of that. Again, what we were exposed to was limited.

What do you think of the remake of the movie being done?

PATT: Are you talking about *Dirty Dancing: Havana Nights*?

No, the one Kenny Ortega is involved with now.

TOM: The one that is going to be made or going to come out?

Yes.

PATT: It would be like remaking *Gone with the Wind*. I mean, I don't even think about it, as a rule. . . . I'm still almost confused or don't understand how people will say, "I've watched it, you know, two hundred times or fifty times." We've watched it maybe—of course when it first came out, we watched it—once or twice. I don't think about it, unless somebody brings it up or something like that.

It is a cult film. It has such a huge following. Leave it alone. Most remakes are not as good. Think of *An Affair to Remember*—Deborah Kerr, Carey Grant—and then Warren Beatty and Annette Bening in *Love Affair*. It just didn't do it. There's only one *Dirty Dancing*. Leave it alone. Let the people love it—have their cult following, fan club, whatever. That would be mine. I think it's just wrong. They may do a wonderful job, but people just care about this film so much.

Why do you think people care about this film so much? Why is *Dirty Dancing* so popular?

PATT: I'm not sure I get it. . . . I think women loved Patrick. I think there had not been kind of a drama-musical around, I guess, maybe in a long time. And you had this young girl, and the love story, and then you had this fabulous dancing.

A movie comes and maybe will last a couple of weeks in a theater. It came to a theater close to where we live. I said, "Tom, I want us to go alone to see this movie when it first comes out." I said, "I'm going to be cool." We went, Sue, with the idea to make a memory. We knew that we could end up never seeing ourselves—end up on the cutting-room floor. We weren't going to be discovered and whisked off to Hollywood. We didn't go with any expectations other than to make a memory for us. And I said, "Okay, I know that we may go through the whole movie and never see ourselves—but if I do, I am going to be very cool about it." So we went to, like, the first showing or something—early afternoon, when there were very few in the theater. And of course, the first time I saw us, I jumped up. I said, "There we are!" If somebody said, "I hear you were in *Dirty Dancing*," we'd say, "Yeah, but don't blink." There were people who called us and said, "Do you know you're in this movie?" Yeah, so [there were] people that did not know that we had done it.

TOM: We're recognizable in the movie. A niece of ours—that did not even know that we were up there participating—went to the movie and jumped up in the middle of the movie and said, "There's Uncle Tommy and Aunt Patt."

PATT: I tell people, "Don't blink."

I don't know the appeal, except it was just at the right time. It appealed to young people. I have never heard a man say, "Oh, you know, I have watched it over and over and over." I have heard men say they liked it. I think it's a chick flick, really. All of the ingredients were—the love story, the dancing. It just caught on. It's one of those things that you almost can't explain.

TOM: I think a movie has chemistry or it doesn't. I think it's awfully difficult to define, because if you could define it, folks would be producing every movie that was made with chemistry. It just has the chemistry—whatever elements—the tension between the various characters and so forth, and the happy, you know, the feel-good kind of story line, and excellent portrayals by each one of the characters. So it just had the right chemistry. Maybe the timing of the movie, you know, when it comes out and what the public is ready for or hungry for, needing, whatever. It was a big surprise.

PATT: It stayed at this theater that we went to something like eight weeks.

TOM: Yep.

PATT: I mean, that's unheard of. They just rotate. Everybody has seen it that wants to see it within a couple of weeks—most movies.

And it was there, like, six or eight weeks. People would just go back and back and back. I couldn't define it.

TOM: Sue, if the movie had never been released, all of our expectations would have been fulfilled. I mean making memories, seeing how movies are made, having some fun, rubbing elbows with the stars, et cetera—that's what we expected. That's what we went there for. We never expected anything else—stardom or discovery or being seen in the movies or whatever. The fact that it became a cult film and the fact that we are actually recognizable in there—albeit just for moments—was all gravy. It's kind of fun and kind of nice. We don't obsess on it. We don't have specialized license plates or anything. We just enjoy these kind of moments—talking to you or whoever might express interest. It was a lot of fun.

PATT: I will tell you, and this came out when I interviewed Eleanor, that those quick scenes when Jennifer would come down and she was practicing by herself on the little bridge, and then she put her lipstick on: That was an afterthought. They had finished. They had wrapped. I guess Eleanor or somebody got the idea. I believe it was, like, a Saturday morning or something like that. Jennifer didn't feel good at all. She was really sick. Eleanor said, "I will give you anything you want if you can pull yourself together and do these fast scenes." And she said they had the clothes and everything right there and they would change into the costumes quickly.

That is such a memorable part of the movie—where she's coming down with her arms up, and she's practicing, and then she comes down and puts her lipstick on and everything. That was an afterthought done after they had supposedly wrapped the movie. And yet people remember that.

How many times did Patrick jump off the stage while practicing the last scene?

TOM: I didn't keep count, but it was a number of times. What would you say, Patt?

PATT: No more than half a dozen.

TOM: Six, eight times.

PATT: He could jump because he studied at the Joffrey Ballet in New York after he left his mother's studio. At this time, remember Patrick was thirty-five years old. When he would jump off, I couldn't even catch my breath—when he would do that, and he landed on his knee and did a twirl. When the camera stopped, he would just almost collapse in pain. At that point in a dancer's life, the knees have had a lot of stress. It would hurt him when he would drop down on his knees. . . . But I guess he did it maybe a half a dozen times.

And the scene I was sorry they did not choose to use was when she goes and she runs and he catches her. The camera was right on her face, but they never use that in the film. All the extras were sitting there and got to see that. I wish that had been in the film because it was really, really neat.

TOM: Sue, I'll share one other thing. Patt's sister, Betty Rollins—Betty and her husband, Jack, live in Birmingham, our home town. We called them up excitedly to tell them that we were going to be in a movie, and Betty's response was, "Not without us, you're not."

PATT: They are dancers, by the way.

TOM: We told the young lady that had signed us up—we contacted her and said, "We have another couple here that are dancers, just like we are." The scheduler said, "Please tell them to come." So they came up and stayed with us for the week. And they show up in the picture as well. I think Betty had on, what, a pink . . .

PATT: A long pink dress. Betty is in the kind of opening dance scene. She is in the right corner. So you see them a couple of times as well.

She was my double. It was a Friday night. We thought it was the last night and we had someplace to go on Saturday that was very important. And we said, "We will not go, if you need us." And they said "No, we're done. We're through with this scene, you can go." We said, "We won't be back," and we said our goodbyes. So Saturday afternoon, they said, "Where are Patt and Tom? We need Patt and Tom. Where are they?"

My sister said, "Look, you told them you did not need them anymore. They are in Durham, North Carolina, but we look very much alike." She said, "Get me a yellow dress." And then they got someone to put on a white dinner jacket. People have noticed that . . . you know, people that look to see the . . .

TOM: Discrepancies.

PATT: And they have said, "It's not the same lady sitting next to the Bungalow Bunny." So, you know, I said, "Oh yes, I had an understudy." She sat in. . . . They assured us that they were not going to do anything else with that scene, and then I guess they needed to reshoot something. So she just took my place.

TOM: I'll make an observation of Patrick. It was my perception that when he came out just to visit (and he did, he'd come out to the extras tent as Patt said earlier, to allow people to get pictures with him and all that), when he was just walking around, you might say not pumped up and in character, and so forth, I didn't see just an ongoing continuous kind of animal magnetism kind of thing—nostrils flaring and all that sort of stuff. He was just sort of—other than being a handsome guy—he was just a regular guy walking around. But when it came time for filming, I just had this image in my head that he was probably in his trailer getting himself pumped up. There was the feeling—that almost perception—that when he came out on the set, there was steam coming out of his nostrils. He was just pumped up and ready to go, and had a totally different persona than when he was relaxed and just walking out amongst all of us extras.

PATT: You do know that it is somewhat autobiographical. Eleanor did do some dancing. She went to the Catskills as a young girl. Part of Eleanor is Jennifer. . . .

They had a big party (they didn't show the film, it wasn't like a premiere), but they had a big party at Lake Lure some months, I guess, after the movie came out, or at some point, and Eleanor was here. Kenny was not. I think she was the only big name that was there. And that's when I got my interview with her. . . .

Maurice Williams & the Zodiacs. . . . And Maurice [who wrote and performed the song "Stay," which is in the movie] happened to be a friend of ours, and I had interviewed him a number of times.

TOM: Patt is an honorary Zodiac.

PATT: He lucked out because his song is on the flip side of Patrick's "She's Like the Wind." Because, you know, that Patrick wrote it and performed "She's Like the Wind," and they had to have something on the flip side, and they chose one of Maurice's songs. I think it was "Stay" because he told me (his wife's name is Emily), he said, "Yep, that was a good one for me, Patt. I bought Emily a Mercedes from that," (from the sale of the record). But you know, they could have chosen any of the music in there because people bought it for Patrick's "She's Like the Wind," and he was just lucky enough, fortunate enough, to be the one chosen to be on the flip side. Maurice is such a nice guy. It couldn't happen to a nicer guy.

Looking at the two of you and dance: Are you trained dancers? How has dance played a role in your relationship?

TOM: Well, we met on the dance floor and we courted on the dance floor. We didn't do as much while we were raising our two children, but then as they got out on their own—and it doesn't take long for kids to grow up and get out—then we got back to dancing. We started taking lessons and getting more formal—not just the stuff that we kind of copied and so forth. Anyway, as our dancing progressed, people started asking us if we were teachers. And eventually we became teachers. We've been teaching dancing for, and this is just informal . . .

PATT: It's an avocation; it is not a vocation.

TOM: We've been teaching dancing for about thirty-two years or so. And so we're just social dancers. That was exactly what they were looking for. We were up for this audition. There was absolutely no organization to it. It was in a dance studio in Hendersonville.

PATT: They didn't say, "Each couple, get up and dance." It was nothing like that. There was music. You got on the dance floor. You danced your dance. And everybody was dancing. It was like going to a club, almost.

TOM: There were people up there dancing far beyond their skill level—attempting to, to do things that they didn't know how to do—trying to show out and all that. We were not into that. We heard some music. We said, "Well, while we are here" (we had already just about decided against participating because we didn't want to sign up for seven days), "we might as well enjoy this nice music." We got up and danced a little bit. Anyway, we were in the process of taking lessons at that time. It's a lifelong thing of taking lessons. You never know it all.

PATT: We have kind of a dance studio in our house. It's really a party room.

TOM: We teach there. We entertain there, and so forth.

PATT: The bathroom downstairs is a Hollywood bathroom: a lot of people I interviewed and a lot of pictures from the film. We have a collage. . . . My sister has a number of pictures. . . . The newspaper did something—it was just a couple of years ago, because we were going to be on the first *Dirty Dancing* Festival panel.

That is how I found you. I saw the article ["Spartanburg's 'Dirty Dancing' extras to share experiences," by Kim Kimzey, GoUpstate.com, September 16, 2010] on the Internet.

PATT: Oh really. It's on the Internet? I think I am in a green jacket outside. . . .

I would love to have some photos for the book.

There is a picture of Jack Weston and me that either I have or my sister has. The BBC came to our house because they did a documentary. . . . They were just over the moon about *Dirty Dancing*, and on the twentieth anniversary, they were doing a documentary and everything. My sister happened to be here, and we had her scrapbook, and I don't have it now, but maybe I can make some copies. . . . They are all our personal photos.

Getting back to Jack Weston.

PATT: I adored him. . . . I said, "Everybody else wants to run away with Patrick. I want to run away with Jack Weston." I just thought he was wonderful. . . .

Was there any romance on the set involving Patrick?

PATT: I didn't see any of that. A lot of people have asked, you know, was there any romance going on with Patrick? Patrick, absolutely not. Of course, we weren't that close, but I didn't see anything going on. It was limited because we couldn't even get to our automobiles. If we wanted to leave, we couldn't. It was almost like being hostages because they took us to this tent, and our cars were somewhere else.

TOM: There would be an assembly point. You drive there and then a bus would carry you around to the set. So we were miles from transportation.

PATT: But you know, our access to anything like that was limited, so nothing was obvious. We will try to get some pictures. . . .

We did have the time of our lives. . . . It was just wonderful. We just went up to make a memory and we enjoyed it. It's kind of fun. It's going to be nice for the grandchildren. I don't know if anybody will ever be able to say what was or is the thing that made it as popular—I mean it is a cult film, period. It's really hard to define why. It is the chemistry. It is Patrick. It is the story. It's so many things, but I don't think you can say it's just one thing. It spoke to you at a time when you were in the one place. For some, it's Patrick, Patrick, Patrick. So it's hard to say. I just have fond memories and I'm so glad that we did it. And it's just fun to relive those memories with someone like you because we do not think about it every day.

Anything else you want to say about Patrick?

PATT: Well, he was really a really nice guy. He didn't seem to have an attitude, which I appreciated.

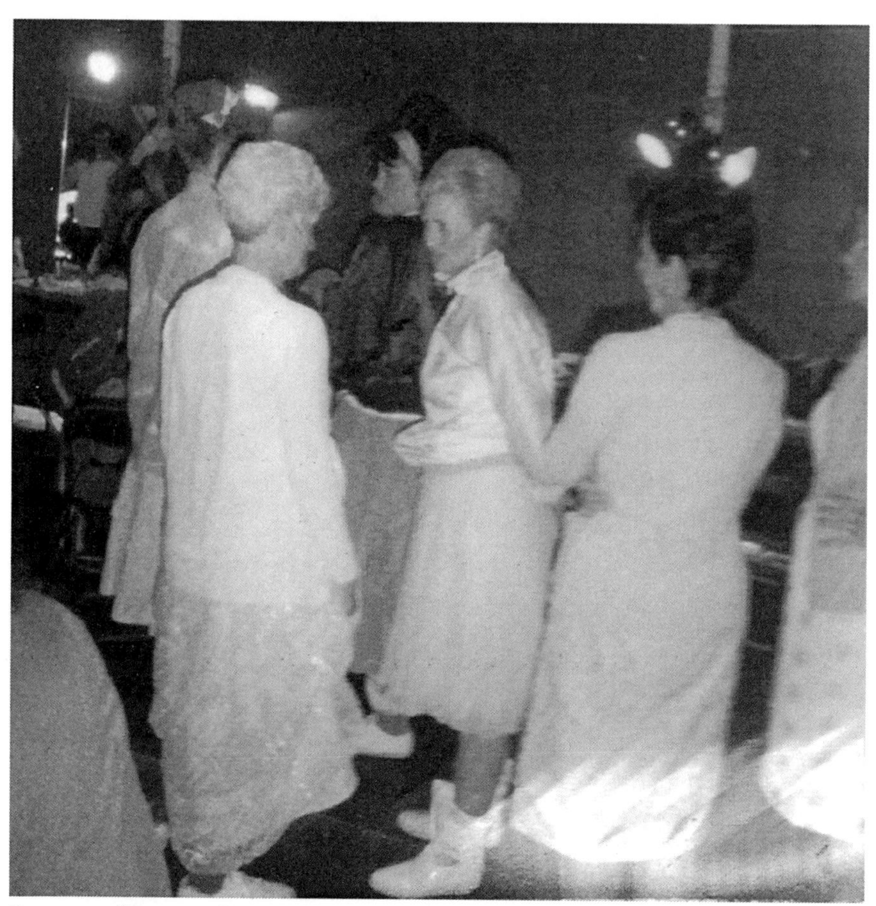

Courtesy of Betty Rollins.

Betty and Patt waiting for makeup.

CHAPTER TEN

BETTY ROLLINS

EXTRA, *DIRTY DANCING*, LAKE LURE FILM LOCATION
Birmingham, Alabama
August 21, 2012 (telephone interview)

How did you find out that they needed extras for the filming of *Dirty Dancing*?

BETTY: Patt, my sister, called me and said that she and Tom [her husband] were going to be in it, and they were going to be extras. Patt and I are very close and I said, "You can't be in there without me. I want to know if we [me and my husband, Jack] can come." So she called them, and the girl called me back and said yes.

So you were in it right from the beginning.

BETTY: Right—at the beginning of Asheville, not in Virginia. I even asked her about the costume and told her what I had, and she said that would be fine.

Did you have to audition?

BETTY: No.

Wow. Okay.

BETTY: I told her, you know, we had been dancing. I don't think they had a lot of professional dancers for extras anyway, in my opinion.

Right. What was your experience with dancing? Were you a social dancer? Were you a dance teacher?

BETTY: We were raised in a family of dancers. My mother and father were ballroom dancers. Actually, my mother was a dancer when she was very young. We did not know that until after she died because at her age that was not necessarily a great profession to be—a dancer on stage (because I think she was in a burlesque-type show). That's another story—a very interesting story. She and my dad danced. He saw her on stage and said he had to meet her. So they danced, and so, consequently, we were raised by a mother and daddy to dress up and go to dances. It was a running joke that you had to dance to get in my family.

My husband—when we met—my husband danced. His mother was a very proper Southern woman and said all young men need to know how to dance. She made him take dance lessons when he was a teenager. He resented it so much—everybody was playing ball and he was taking ballroom lessons. He said he looks back and he's so glad he did. We started taking round dancing—that's where ballroom dancing is done in a circle. They call the steps out and you do them in ballroom fashion. They're international steps. They're harder than you would get from a ballroom teacher. So we did it for, I guess, twenty-five or thirty years. We traveled all over the United States, almost, doing that.

We started teaching some just in the Birmingham area. We went to the Cloister for fourteen years and took some teachers down there. And actually that's where Jack White was after *Dirty Dancing* was over. He was one of the people who helped teach up in Asheville. We didn't know that until, actually, we started going to the Cloister. And we became good friends. Yes, we've danced forever. . . . We quit teaching about three years ago.

What scenes were you guys in?

BETTY: We were in the audience when Patrick Swayze was (of course) dancing with Jennifer. In the audience, Jack has a white tuxedo coat and I have on a long, pink evening gown—probably the only long dress that was there. They came and took the camera stand and it came right at me and I don't think you see Jack as much in that. I turned my face and looked at him. When the Bungalow Bunny got angry and stood up and walked out, then they showed Jack. He was sitting right behind her when she got up. So you will see him in his white coat.

Patt and Tom had to leave two days before it was over. They had another commitment. So they moved Jack's seat, and he might have taken Tom's seat. I stayed where I was. We were almost parallel to the table where Jennifer Grey and her "parents" were sitting.

Oh, wow!

BETTY: We were in that row. When the girl got up to leave, we were right there by her.

It was very interesting because the only, I guess, personal thing that we had to do with anybody there—let me back up. Patt, of course, at that time was in TV, so she talked to some of them outside of their trailers and so forth, and I would see them, but I had nothing to say. Kenny [Ortega] and Emile [Ardolino] both came up to us and thanked Jack and I for staying and cooperating—which was very personal. I thought it was great. "Thank you. You all are wonderful. You've been through it all with us."

Then the writer, Eleanor Bergstein, came up to Jack and me and thanked us. I said, "Well, you know, it's just an experience. We've enjoyed it. It's different. We know we may not be in it. We could be on the cutting-room floor. We understood that when we came in." She said, "I guarantee you that you will be seen in this movie." She was a neat lady. I liked her—very down-to-earth. Of course, all of them were busy. She was very, very sweet to Jack and me.

Wow.

BETTY: I mean, it's just a flash. You know they cut it down for the TV. In the movie, it's wider and you can see Jack and me dancing in the movie. But on the video, on the right-hand side, you can see me in the long pink dress—right in the corner of the right-hand side of the video—right at the end when everybody's dancing.

I am going to go watch that and look for you. That is amazing. Did you have any contact with Patrick Swayze at all?

BETTY: I did not. Patt did. He hurt his knee and so he was out a couple of times. He stayed very much to himself.

I did meet Cynthia Rhodes. Her mother and father were from Nashville, so they came up and spent a couple of nights up there while we were filming. Of course, being Southerners, they were darling and very warm and friendly. She was very warm. I never saw Jennifer. And of course, the band leader was wonderful. Like I said, Patt rolled around a little bit more and talked to them more than I did at the time.

Fortunately, we took a few pictures. . . . I am sorry I did not take more. . . . Some of them were costume and makeup at six o'clock in the morning. It showed us dancing in the tents waiting to be called. . . . I think there's one of me with Jack Weston.

Oh my gosh.

BETTY: There's one with me talking to him and one with Patt talking to him. I danced with Kenny.

Oh!

BETTY: He came up and said something. I said, "You can have my paycheck if I can just dance a few steps with you." He said, "You can keep it." And we danced. It was wonderful. I said I would rather dance with him than Patrick almost.

Really.

BETTY: Fabulous! Fabulous!

It was horrible weather. We were freezing. Freezing cold rain. And if you've seen any of the interviews from Jack. . . . He was on Jay Leno. He said, for him, it was a terrible experience. The weather was terrible. It was wet. They had to bring in these huge, huge fans to even warm the tent. The dancers—what we called the street dancers, you know, that were in the movie—some of those people would come down and we would do, like, a *Soul Train* line. And they had long, like, church tables where you would seat twelve or fifteen people. Of course, they'd get in the middle and they'd start a *Soul Train* line. They were darling. They would come and mix and mingle with us. I mean, we had to do something to take up the time. Otherwise, we were sleeping.

Did Patt tell you she put names to everybody?

There was a lady in the red dress. What was she named: Elizabeth Taylor?

BETTY: She was a hair stylist, so she did everybody's nails and everything, for like five dollars, just to pass the time. Then she was giving pedicures and manicures to the stars.

There was a guy there who was an excellent dancer, and he would dance with two of us at a time. He could lead two women.

But overall, I would say it was a very hard ten days because of the rain. They were having money problems. I don't know whether Patt told you.

Yes, she did.

BETTY: They didn't know what they were going to do. So they were trying to wrap it up as quickly as they could or at least have enough money to go the extra few days to wrap it up. I think there was some tension there. That was just hearsay on my part. . . .

Would I do it again? Probably. I don't know, the last few days—we thought we would only be there, like, seven days, and it ended up being ten days. Patt and Tom had something to do that last weekend, and Jack and I stayed on. It was difficult weather—terrible, terrible weather. And of course, we did not stay at Lake Lure. We went back to Patt's a couple nights, but we decided it was just too long a drive, so we stayed at a motel up there.

That's why I said I didn't really have that much to tell you.

Oh, yes you did.

BETTY: We never got involved, you know, with the stars, so to speak. The waiter, who was the bad guy, would come out and was very pleasant.

The guy who played Robbie [Max Cantor]?

BETTY: Yes. He came out and talked to us. And like I said, Cynthia came out and talked and just mingled.

They had food tables out all the time for us. Then, the last night, when it was a wrap, they had pizza come in, and everybody had pizza because it was twelve-thirty at night, on Saturday night, that we wrapped. There was always something to nibble on. You had to do something to pass the time or be bored out of your mind.

And we had a guy who would walk around the tent and steal.

Steal?

BETTY: I had some rhinestone earrings stolen. I saw him. I didn't see him pick them up. He would just walk around the tables and pick up anything he wanted. Which I thought was kind of interesting.

Was he an extra?

BETTY: Yes, he was an extra. Somebody said, "Be careful. There's somebody picking up things." Then I put the earrings down and I thought, surely he wouldn't. But then I saw him walking around and they were gone. I guess that in itself—just the different people that were there. And some took it very seriously.

I mean, after all—as you know, probably—when you're in costumes, you can have holes in dresses, and splits, and from the stage you can't tell what things look like. We had just started. I guess the first day of the thing, this blonde came out and she said, "Sir, sir, there's a split under my arm." And I'll never forget, Kenny said, "Well, then just keep your arm down."

I love it.

BETTY: I loved it. I thought, "Lady, you don't even know whether your arm will be in the show."

That is too funny. I have a new question: Why do you think *Dirty Dancing* has been so popular? I mean, it's the twenty-fifth anniversary—right now.

BETTY: I have tried to figure it out because when I came back, I had people whisper, "She was in *Dirty Dancing*. She was in *Dirty Dancing*." The housekeeper came up to me, and she's, I guess, in her late forties, early fifties, and she said, "That is my husband's favorite movie."

Really.

BETTY: "He looks at it over and over again." And I thought, "Okay, he was a teenager. By golly, we'll dance any way we want to"—which was the theme of the movie. We looked down our noses at that kind of dancing. I think it must have been an era where children broke free and just said, "We'll dance the way we want to." I think that's exactly what they did. You know the name of the movie was supposed to be *I Had the Time of My Life*.

Oh, really? I hadn't heard that.

BETTY: And then they changed it. We did not know what the name of the movie was going to be when we got up there. And I don't know that I even knew it was going to be *Dirty Dancing*. So we thought it was going to be the name of the title of the song. I just think, at that time, that just attracted: What are they going to be doing in there? I think it was just the thing—the older people, the parents called it dirty dancing, because, of course, that's not the way we danced. I think it was just kind of a rebellion.

But I ask myself: "Why would that hokey movie be the sensation that it's been? Why didn't I draw my twenty-five dollars out and invest in it?" When they wanted money so badly. You know, I thought: "Oh my goodness, who would have thought?"

So what do you think about the remake of the movie that Kenny Ortega is directing? It's supposed to come out in 2014.

BETTY: Tell me about that. I've heard just some little something, but we've been in the midst of moving.

Kenny Ortega is supposed to be the director of a remake of *Dirty Dancing*. What happened was they have not cast the parts of the two main leads: for Johnny—Patrick's role—or for Baby—Jennifer's role. So now the movie has been put on hold for awhile. I was reading the other day, they had their film locations and the dirty dancers and all that.

A lot of the fans were really upset because when they made the announcement, it had not been that long since Patrick died. A lot of people think they'll never make a movie as good as the original one. And once again, who is going to play the main characters?

Would you go see a remake?

BETTY: I doubt it. I don't see it in my head, and I thought about it—that's funny when I first heard they could do a remake, what would they do with it? It was a summer romance. . . . How could they have brought those people back together?

I think they're just going to have the same story and just have younger actors and actresses in it. I think, certain movies, they should just leave them alone.

BETTY: How many of the second movies are as good as the first ones? To me, that movie had a purpose—whether it was shallow or whatever. It was just the beginning of a different era. The music is not the same as it ever was—so that had a point as far as the kind of music. So I don't know what they could do. Maybe my imagination just isn't big enough. It would never be as popular as *Dirty Dancing*. . . . To tell you the truth, Sue, I don't get it.

We just moved into a retirement home and they've asked us to teach dancing here.

Excellent.

BETTY: We have to do something. Jack and I are still very active for our age. . . . Everybody is impressed: "Oh, you were in that wonderful movie." I thought, "That hokey movie." That's kind of the way I see it. If you get down to it, it was about the music and dancing—the kids rebelling or wanting their own style. Am I seeing it right?

Everybody sees it in their own way. I don't think there's one right way to see it, you know. How many times have you watched it?

BETTY: I don't know that I've ever watched it completely—maybe three times. I watched it the first time. I have never necessarily liked to perform. . . . I watched it and it made me nervous to think: "Oh my goodness, I'm going to be on TV." And yet I did it.

Right. I was wondering if I could ever do anything like that. I'm not a dancer, but, you know, just being a regular extra—that would be scary.

BETTY: . . . It was an experience. . . . People are very, very in awe of me being in that movie.

I am. I'm one of those people in awe.

BETTY: It was interesting to see it made. It was interesting to see the cameras. I was fascinated how they carry the cameras on their stomach and move around the dancers with the cameras on their bodies.

I remember when we first got there, Cynthia and Patrick were doing the scene where they were on the dance floor, and they told them to stop. Kenny had them stop, and he said, "You're too harsh with that, Cynthia." Something like that. I know with the street dancers at the end, when they were all moving toward Patrick in the end, he told them, "You're over-dancing. Cool down." So it was interesting to see the direction.

Miranda—the Bunny—she was a fantastic dancer. She and Kenny would dance and sometimes get together and dance across the floor—whether they were trying to show Patrick or Jennifer something. It was nice to see them dance. . . .

Kenny was a neat guy. . . . I think he was so pleasant.

It's a very sad situation that all of them that had such a part of it are gone. Of course, Jennifer is still around. Cynthia, of course, married [Richard Marx] and sang with her husband's band. . . . She was neat and warm and so forth, and her family was adorable.

Courtesy of Betty Rollins.

Betty and Eleanor Bergstein. In the background are Kenny Ortega (left) and Patrick Swayze (right).

Courtesy of Betty Rollins.

Betty and Emile Ardolino.

Courtesy of Betty Rollins.

Patrick Swayze walking his dog.

Courtesy of Betty Rollins.

Patrick Swayze and extras in the ballroom.

Courtesy of Betty Rollins.

Cynthia Rhodes and extras.

Courtesy of Betty Rollins.

Betty and Kenny Ortega.

Courtesy of Betty Rollins.

Patt and Jack Weston.

Courtesy of Betty Rollins.

Betty and Jack Weston.

Courtesy of Betty Rollins.

Betty and Cynthia Rhodes.

Courtesy of Betty Rollins.

Patt and Max Cantor.

Courtesy of Betty Rollins.

Betty and Honi Coles.

Courtesy of Betty Rollins.

Patt and Betty having hair done.

Courtesy of Betty Rollins.

Tom Rocks with sign used for local premiere party.

OPEN CALL

DANCING FILM PRODUCTIONS, INC.

WELCOME!! Thank you for coming to our open call. We are casting for extras to be in the movie DANCING! which is shooting in the Blacksburg area September 5-19, 1986.

DANCING! starring Patrick (The Outsiders) Swayze and Jennifer (Ferris Bueller's Day Off) Grey, is the story of a young girl's summer in the Catskills in 1963 in a glamourous family resort where she falls in love with a handsome young dance instructor from "the other side of the tracks," learns to dance, and grows into a responsible and mature young woman.

If you are chosen to be in our movie, you can expect a phone call sometime within the next week or two. You will be expected to provide your own transportation to and from the location. You will be paid a small stipend per day, and fed lunch.

In filling out our questionnaire, please give as many telephone numbers as you can, including friends, neighbors, parents, and workplaces where we might be able to leave a message. The easier you are to reach, the better chance you have of being in the movie. Please include the best times to be reached at these numbers.

Also indicate your general schedule, and if it is flexible. This way if we need somebody at the last minute, we'll know who to call.

If you accept a job as an extra, there are a few things you should know about the "job."

1. Filming starts early and runs long -- generally 12-14 hours -- so do not accept a call as an extra unless your whole day is free.

2. If you cannot make the day or days you are scheduled for, please give us a call, otherwise we will be counting on you. DO NOT send your husband, wife, or neighbor instead -- you've been chosen for a specific scene for a reason.

3. If you are called for a wardrobe fitting, please bring the items you have listed on the wardrobe list to the fitting with you. Remember, this is 1963, not the 80's, so don't check those items unless they seem period (think Jackie Kennedy and Sandra Dee). MEN: You will need to get your hair cut, so be prepared for that.

4. You will be asked to call us the afternoon or the evening before you work (that's when we tell you the specifics of where to report and at what time). If our lines are busy, please keep trying, as we are talking to alot of people!

5. Again, thank you for coming, and as soon as you've filled out the questionnaire completely, please get in line to have your picture taken.

Thank you, and we look forward to working with you!!

Credit: Courtesy of Mountain Lake Hotel.

CHAPTER ELEVEN

BETTY ROLLINS INTERVIEWS SUE TABASHNIK

At the end of my interview with Betty on August 21, 2012, she asked me questions regarding how I became interested in writing my first book (which was published in 2010). In the course of answering her questions, I spoke about my experiences meeting Patrick Swayze and traveling to one of the primary film locations, Mountain Lake Hotel in Virginia.

BETTY: Tell me about this book. How did you get interested in writing about this? What fascinates you?

You know what—I've always loved the movies. What happened was, when *Dirty Dancing* came out in 1987, I went to see it, like I went to a lot of movies. It just really struck a chord with me because, at the time, I had just broken up with a guy who I thought was my soul mate for life. It was a really tough time. Somehow or other, when I went to the movie, it just really perked me up. I had seen Patrick Swayze in the TV movie *North and South*, but I think I only watched part of it. I wasn't that into it, but he really interested me in *Dirty Dancing*. So I went back a couple more times to see *Dirty Dancing*. Then I saw Patrick Swayze when he was interviewed by Barbara Walters—that was, like, in 1988. I don't know if you saw it.

BETTY: Yeah.

He broke down when he was talking about his father, and that very much impressed me because he seemed very genuine.

BETTY: He adored his father. I think he really did have an attachment to his father.

Yeah. Then he impressed me because of his marriage. So I started watching more interviews and reading about him and stuff like that. At that point, I actually received an autographed picture of him sent from the US fan club. I always went to all of his movies—no matter what he was in.

BETTY: So your fascination was with him.

Yeah. In 2000, I bought a computer finally, and while on the Internet, I found the Official Patrick Swayze International Fan Club and I joined. I thought this might be really hokey or something stupid, but it turned out to be a great experience. I became very active in the club. The club president, Margaret Howden, actually lives in Scotland. The club still goes on. I ended up meeting Patrick four times.

BETTY: You did!

I live near Detroit—very near. Patrick came here to Detroit with a dance company, Complexions. He was on the board of directors, and his wife, Lisa, was also. He came to host a fundraiser. The company is based out of New York, and they have dancers in the company from all over the world. They do outreach with inner city kids. They came to Detroit twice, and he came with them twice. That was in 2002 and 2004. He did not dance, but he introduced the dance company—they danced. Then he hosted a benefit reception afterward, at which proceeds from the ticket sales were given to the dance company. At the benefit reception, he gave pictures and autographs and all that stuff. So that was forty-five minutes from where I live.

The other two times were kind of through the fan club. He and his wife, Lisa, they did a movie, *One Last Dance*. I don't know if you've ever seen it.

BETTY: No, I'd love to see it.

You could rent it from Blockbuster or something. Oh my gosh. I love that movie. That was their passion. They had originally done a stage show in Beverly Hills, and then they wanted to turn it into a movie, and it took them, I don't know, like, twenty years to do it or something. Lisa wrote it. She was the director. She was the star. Patrick was the star. They had another dancer—George de la Peña—who was the third star in the movie. Lisa and Patrick were also each a producer. [The movie told the story of dancers from the dancers' point of view with the theme that it is never too late to realize your dreams.]

It premiered in Houston—that's where Patrick and Lisa were from—at the WorldFest-Houston International Film Festival in 2003. People from the club—like around twenty-five to thirty people—flew in from Europe, all over the States, and other places. We got to see the movie. We were sitting right near Patrick's and Lisa's families. The movie was playing in four theaters all at the same time. Patrick and Lisa introduced the movie, and then afterward they had a champagne reception. Patrick was running all over the place with minimal security and no bodyguards.

BETTY: Weren't you thrilled out of your mind?

Oh my God. At the premiere, he gave special pictures for the fan club members—like group pictures—in addition to the individual pictures. The next day, we were going on a bus tour to see where Patrick's school, childhood home, and church were and other places that he had frequented. I thought this was kind of a little hokey.

BETTY: I love it.

Well, listen to this. So who comes on to the bus? His mom, Patsy. Okay. And then she says something like, "Well, Patrick is going to come on the bus, and we're going to talk to you, and you can ask anything you want. Patrick asks, could you please not take any pictures because he did give you a lot of pictures last night." Everyone is like, "Oh my goodness, oh my goodness. Of course we won't take pictures."

So he came on the bus, and he and his Mom talked to us for about forty-five minutes. Honestly, I was sitting, like, in the third row. We didn't know this was going to happen. It was a surprise. Margaret Howden arranged it. I got a question off and I was so nervous and excited that I could hardly listen to the answer.

BETTY: But you got your question off.

It was so amazing. And then I went to the Nashville Film Festival in 2004 to see *One Last Dance* again. I met up with two ladies, Jan Griffith and Shirley Penrod, from Texas from the fan club. I had never met them. Margaret Howden had told Patrick's personal assistant at the time that we were going to be there. So, to make a long story short, after we saw the movie and Patrick and Lisa had given a Question-and-Answer session and all that, they were at a jazz club eating dinner in the basement.

We were able—nobody else but us three ladies—were able to go over to where they were after they finished their dinner and talk with Patrick and Lisa. And then the personal assistant took our three cameras and took pictures of all of us with Patrick and Lisa. I talked to Patrick one-on-one for about three minutes. I said goodbye to Patrick, and he goes and gives me a big bear hug and says, "Thank you so much for coming." He gave bear hugs to the other two ladies also. He was very humble, very gracious, very nice.

BETTY: Well, you just fell in love with him.

I did. I really liked basically what he stood for: traditional values, the work ethic, integrity. Of course, he's not bad to look at.

BETTY: To watch him dance just blew my mind. I mean, you know, the moves and so forth. . . .

In *One Last Dance*, Bambi [Patrick's sister] is one of the dancers. Patrick's mom, Patsy*, is one of the four choreographers. It was just kind of like a life dream. It went right to DVD, but I understand that a lot of the dance schools show it. . . . I've been watching it a lot lately. I tear up. They have a behind-the-scenes segment where they interview Lisa and Patrick about making the movie. . . .

Back to my writing my book, I was just fascinated by: Why did so many people fall in love with *Dirty Dancing*? I'm a full-time social worker in real life. To me, it was fascinating. I was very active in the club. I started my first book in 2007, before Patrick was diagnosed. It became a bittersweet experience for me.

I went to Virginia to Mountain Lake Hotel in 2009 because Buzz Scanland, the manager, invited me to go there. It was so sweet. I was going to interview him on the telephone. "No. No. You have to come here." It was in January—six below zero. So I didn't even stay there because I was by myself, and it was so cold and off-season. So I stayed at the Holiday Inn [which, actually, in 1986 had been a hotel by a different name, and some cast and crew members during the filming of *Dirty Dancing* stayed there]. Buzz would pick me up and take me up the mountain and show me all of the archives and the locations where various scenes were shot. He showed the movie on a big screen in the recreation area for me, and I remember just sitting there crying while watching it.

**Patsy Swayze, an amazing person, passed on September 16, 2013. Her lifework and spirit will continue to touch many, many people.*

He drove me around the property, pointing out where various scenes were filmed. I walked around outside and took a lot of pictures.

BETTY: You've had some wonderful experiences.

Yes. I have met so many wonderful people.

CHAPTER TWELVE

FAN TRIBUTES TO *DIRTY DANCING*

ANNA MATHIAS

Age 38
Budapest, Hungary
March 15, 2012

The Time of My Life

Well, let me write you my feelings about the movie. When I listen to the radio and hear the music of "The Time of My Life" (final dance), at times, it is a real time-travel into the past, where I was a teen and I had an easy and unworried life with less responsibility. (It doesn't mean that at the moment I'm not happy or satisfied, since I have a wonderful 2-year-old daughter, and I would never reverse the present for the past just to take its advantages. I could never imagine my life without my daughter.)

Listening to the rhythm of "The Time of My Life," I can relive impressions of youth life with holidays, independence, love, truth, music, and lots of dance. Aside from the smile of my daughter, the *DD* feeling gives me, too, the strength I need to be able to cope with everyday problems. Whenever I am listening to this music, I recall the steps of the final dance, and if the circumstances permit it, I try to follow suit and have the time of my life.

DEBBIE WALLERSTEIN

Age 58
Palm Beach, Florida
April 24, 2012

25 Years? That Can't Be Right!

So much has changed. 25 years ago, as I sat in the darkened Massapequa Theater day after day finding refuge from devastating illness, I didn't have even the smallest clue about how big this little movie would become.

All I knew then was that, for a little while each day, I could forget the pain and depression and spend time with my new friends, Baby and Johnny, in a world where anything was possible and happy endings existed.

I could enjoy beautiful dancing that wasn't part of a classic old movie and wasn't performed by dancers who were now aging or (worse) dead. These dancers were young, vibrant, and just as gorgeous as Fred, Gene, Ginger, and Cyd.

Today, 25 years later, I look back at that time and smile. Because despite the incredibly horrible state of my health, what I remember most clearly is the joy I felt each day as I sat in that theater.

I feel such immense gratitude to Linda Gottlieb, Vestron Pictures, and the entire cast and crew for helping me through such an awful time in my life.

And I feel a great sadness about all of those people who are no longer here. Dr. Houseman—gone. Max Kellerman—gone. And Johnny. . . . How can Patrick Swayze be gone? He was young—only my age, for God's sake! That is so not right!

Now, when I hear a song from the movie or catch it on television, I am filled with incredible sadness right along with my love of the movie. Since Patrick's death, I have not been able to watch any of his films except *Dirty Dancing*.

So I hope to see a 25th-anniversary theatrical re-release, because I thoroughly enjoyed those that commemorated the 10- and 20-year anniversaries. What a joy it was to watch audiences of all ages enjoy a film that meant so much to me!

I suppose I could wax philosophical about the triumph of the underdog, finding one's inner beauty, snobs getting their comeuppance, but I will leave that for others.

Just like when I went to a 70th-anniversary theatrical showing of *Casablanca* and a 10th-anniversary showing of the three *Lord of the Rings* movies, the 25th anniversary of *Dirty Dancing* will mean a happy evening with old friends who make me feel good. And isn't that what a good movie is supposed to do?

ELLY ALI

Age 21
Melbourne, Australia
March 20, 2012

Taking It Back to Where It All Began

What the 25th anniversary means to me:

The 25th anniversary of *DD* means quite a lot. Considering it was a very low-budget movie, to thinking that nobody would ever see it, it's amazing how that whole concept changed and made the cast overnight international superstars and the movie a big hit, as well as a household name. It's a great achievement, and the fact it's still popular after so many years is a great representation of just how many people were inspired by it and watch it.

What the movie really means to me:

This movie is by far my favourite movie ever made, what it symbolizes and just the story in general is very natural, and a typical young girl's life as a teenager, going through changes and cutting ties with family, accepting people from different parts of society, knowing what matters and what doesn't in life, and learning values and lessons in life that are important.

What I like about *DD* and the impact it has on me:

I like *DD* so much because I just do. As I've mentioned in the past, it's a very symbolic and sassy love story that in today's world would never happen. I can say one thing, though (it's every girl's essential for her suitcase), it's impacted my life by going back to being 17 years old, the changes you discover in yourself, breaking away and individuating on your own, not wanting to let your parents down, always being the good girl who does the right thing by everybody.

I'm now 21 years old and I feel I've achieved more than what I would have back when I was 17. The older you get, the more you discover what the true things in life can be, and where they take you is an interesting journey that I will fulfill.

HEIDI NIELSEN

June 11, 2012

It's taken me quite a while to put into words what *Dirty Dancing* means to me. From the surface, *Dirty Dancing* is a cute romantic drama with some great music and an attractive lead. Who wouldn't like it? But when I delve into the roots of why I've loved *Dirty*

Dancing for so long, I realize that *Dirty Dancing* sits atop my favorite movie list because it has deep, multi-faceted meanings to me. When I was young, *Dirty Dancing* was a fun love story where the "not so pretty" girl stole the heart of the "bad boy." It was the soundtrack that I listened to on long family car rides and the movie I would play when my girlfriends spent the night. I can't recall the first time I saw the movie—it's as if *Dirty Dancing* has always been a part of me.

As I grew older, I wanted to be just like Baby—smart, witty, and a great dancer. I wanted to be on center stage and show that I had so much more to offer than anyone realized. I would watch *Dirty Dancing* and try to act out the dance moves in my bedroom. The love story between Baby and Johnny became my idea of the ideal love story. With time, *Dirty Dancing* became a coming-of-age story that I related to. I've found myself in Baby's shoes—falling for the "bad boy" and making decisions that felt right in my heart, even if it defied my parents' wishes. *Dirty Dancing* comforted me as I grew from the quiet girl to become a strong, confident woman. This movie has been my shoulder to cry on, my confidant, and my nonjudgmental friend. It's difficult to explain the meaning this movie has to me because the meaning changes so frequently.

Dirty Dancing has also been a lesson in humility, empathy, and equality. Baby falls for Johnny with no regard to social class or education. I've tried to model myself on these principles and look for the best in everyone. *Dirty Dancing* will always hold a special place in my heart. I feel connected to the movie because it's grown deeper as I've grown. With time, I believe my connection with *Dirty Dancing* will only grow—it will become a movie about family values and how times may change, but families and love prevail.

HOLLY TUELL

Age 61
Green Bay, Wisconsin
March 27, 2012

What the 25th anniversary of *Dirty Dancing* means to me:

It means I was 36 when this movie was made! Where does the time go?

What *Dirty Dancing* means to me:

It takes me back to a time in my life that was very similar. There has never been a movie more tuned in to what life was like in the '60s than *Dirty Dancing*. And I know there are many people who are transported back in time when they watch this movie.

Why is *Dirty Dancing* so popular after 25 years?

Because it has survived the test of time. Not only are people from my age group avid fans of this movie, but it has gone on to become a favorite of girls in every age group. In fact, I have a 4-year-old granddaughter, Paige, who will be seeing this movie with Grandma when she's old enough. So many girls, after seeing the movie, had a crush on Johnny Castle (and Patrick Swayze), and yearned to be Baby Houseman.

What I like about *Dirty Dancing*:

As I said earlier, it takes me back to a time in my life where a very similar romance occurred. Only difference was, he was a singer with a band, rather than a dancer at a resort. But much of the rest of the story is the same. . . . Though I married someone else that I love very much, I don't think you ever forget that first magical romance and the magic that came with it!!!

How *Dirty Dancing* has impacted my life:

It renewed my faith in youth and innocence. And it truly introduced me to the wonderful talents of Patrick Swayze and Jennifer Grey. I know they are talking about doing a remake of *Dirty Dancing*, but for me, there will never be a remake that will be able to equal the chemistry and excitement of the original. And there will never be another Johnny and Baby like Patrick and Jennifer. I've talked to people who went to see the remake of *Footloose*, and they said they will stick to the original, with Kevin Bacon and Lori Singer. I am thinking that will be the case with a *DD* remake!

INGRID MENNELLA

Age 56
St. Inverness, Florida
April 17, 2012

Patrick Continues to Inspire Me

I was born in 1956. My childhood amusements were after-school activities, sports, music lessons, and going to the movies. I completely relate to the themes and innuendos in the film *Dirty Dancing* because I lived there—in that time period. There was no talking back to your parents, sex before marriage was not acceptable, and families vacationed together. Young people rebelled by smoking, drinking, and "dirty dancing" because those were things their parents would never approve of; and as I look back I think of those things as harmless fun.

I think the movie still has appeal today, generations later, because our young people today have no outlet for "harmless fun." Hardly anyone writes letters and drops them in the mailbox—we text, instant message, email, or call on the cell phone or Skype. Kids don't go to the drive-in anymore. They play Angry Birds, or some other warrior games on Wii machines, computers, and cell phones. A great number of children come from single-family households who probably never had a family vacation, and what 16-year-old doesn't want a car?

The world is a much less personal place because of all our technology. You can have an "office" meeting on the Internet with people all over the world at the same time. Kids text in a language all their own. The point is, there is much less personal contact in our lives today. There is very little face-to-face time because of all these wonderful technologies. However, our life is sped up to such a fast pace, I feel we have lost the art of conversation and personal interaction. Many families don't sit down for a meal together. A lot of kids stay out all hours and don't function within their family. A lot of kids have no boundaries in place, or rebel violently if they do. I think that's where the movie *Dirty Dancing* comes in. The premise of the film is so apparent and uncomplicated; it's a movie you can watch for sheer enjoyment and not have to pick apart to find its hidden meaning. Life seems to slow down as we watch a family enjoy each other's company and watch a young girl experience her first crush. The purity of the fun and romance is refreshing and probably a little corny to young people today . . . but they watch the film because it makes them feel better . . . they just don't know why.

I love the film because it reminds me of my own childhood. I love the music and the dancing, but more than that I like the simplicity of life at that time, when the worst thing a girl had to worry about was getting a date for the prom. I watch the movie over and over. I love being transported back to the times I wrote in my diary, rolled my hair, was expected to be dressed appropriately for dinner, and rode my bike everywhere. Today's young people don't know what that's like, and I think it's a shame because they don't know what they're missing.

KELLY MINER

Age 41
Southfield, Michigan
April 17, 2012

Still Dancing after 25 Years

Just like the theme song in the movie says: "I had the time of my life." Wow, it's hard to believe I was 16 years old when the movie made its debut. Now I'm 41 and still have special memories of this movie. The 25th anniversary of this movie means to continue to celebrate the nostalgia that this movie brings to both new and old audiences. It's definitely a must-see movie that I would show my younger family relatives, like my 17- and 23-year-old nephews. It's a movie that can be seen several times, and each time you still enjoy and feel the compassionate story line.

That is why I think *Dirty Dancing* is so popular after 25 years. Since the beginning, the movie created a strong following from both dancers and non-dancers alike. I am not a professional dancer, but after watching this movie time and time again, it makes me think I can dance just like the characters in the movie.

Dirty Dancing impacted and continues to impact my life because it opens up a dialog with people who I probably would never come in contact with, yet we share a common bond for being fans of this movie. For me, it's a movie that crosses over all age groups, all races, genders, and nationalities.

Even to this day, *Dirty Dancing* provides an outlet of hope, overcoming adversity, and the music in the movie and type of dirty dancing still resonates with audiences, just like you're seeing it for the very first time.

Dirty Dancing remains an uplifting and inspiring movie about family, love, and it shows what perseverance looks like. *Dirty Dancing* also taught me that, no matter what obstacles you face in life, always take the time to dance and appreciate your life, because after 25 years I am still dancing.

SHIRLEY PENROD

Age range: 60s
Houston, Texas
June 6, 2012

I remember *Dirty Dancing* being released in 1987, but I thought to myself, "Who would want to see a movie about dancing that is 'dirty?'" So I never saw it. I didn't know who Patrick Swayze was back then and didn't see any of his movies that were released in the late '80s. I remember seeing previews for *Ghost*, and that one sounded interesting due to its spiritual component, so I went to see it. I came to know and love Patrick in the years after seeing *Ghost*, *City of Joy*, and *Three Wishes*.

It must have been the mid '90s when I became injured and wound up spending many days and evenings on the couch watching movies. I had purchased *Dirty Dancing* by that time and really enjoyed it. I was intrigued by the concept, loved the singing, and was wild about all of the dancing. I was enthralled with Patrick's sensuous performance and loved the story between him and Baby. I also loved the locations, but had no idea they really existed. I started watching *Dirty Dancing* more and more after that because it lifted my spirits and made me very happy.

I didn't see *Dirty Dancing* in the theater until it was re-released in 2007 for its 20th anniversary. It played at a local theater in Houston, and I saw it twice, two nights in a row. Needless to say, I loved seeing it on the big screen and finally understood why so many female fans were so enthralled with Patrick and his performance. I guess I've watched *Dirty Dancing* at least fifty times since then, but I also watch all of Patrick's movies. Each one inspires and entertains me in different ways. *Dirty Dancing* will always be my absolute favorite. I have four copies of *DD* because every time it is re-released on DVD, I buy a copy—and probably always will whenever a new anniversary edition is released.

The biggest impact *DD* had in my life was inspiring me to learn how to dance. I really enjoyed learning the mambo and had the opportunity to tell Patrick that when I met him for the first time in 2004. Unfortunately, I subsequently learned that I have two left feet (in fact, that was the theme of my first dance class), and after taking several mambo and other Latin dance classes, gave them up because I was so bad and couldn't handle all of the spins without getting terribly dizzy. I still have fond memories of my classes and would never have taken them had it not been for Patrick's influence in my life.

I traveled to Nashville, Tennessee, in 2004 to the Nashville Film Festival to see *One Last Dance*. That was the first time I got to meet Patrick and Lisa as well as Stacy Widelitz. I also got to meet Sue Tabashnik during the trip, and we have kept in touch and been friends ever since. I have Patrick to thank for that.

After that trip, I learned more and more about Patrick and was fortunate to meet him and Lisa three separate times after that. Patrick's passion, intensity, integrity, and love for life made a big impression on me and have inspired me in small ways to live by his example. I have photos of me with him and Lisa, both at home and in my office, and they continue to warm my heart and make me grateful that I knew him. I owe it to Patrick that I have met so many good friends all over the world who are his fans, and continue to love him as much as I do.

TANYA HOLLIDAY

Age 41
Arizona
April 20, 2012

Dirty Dancing. Ah, let me take myself back into time and relive the first time I saw the film. To me, it was a film that just about everyone could relate to. Whether it is of first love, family issues, and even honor—or lack thereof.

I remember seeing the previews and seeing Patrick. Oh my. He was so gorgeous in that film, and what girl doesn't like a good-looking guy that can dance! Dancing is intimate; if you're a guy reading this—girls love it! So, you might want to go and learn! Patrick could dance. He made this movie so sexy! I mean it was so sexy that it was very erotic without having to be like most films today that show so much skin, it makes you uncomfortable to see it in a theater.

I love that time period too. It was of family closeness, going on vacation, and enjoying simple things in life that make you smile and be entertained. It wasn't perfect, but it showed how people were there to help each other out of a bad situation, and how being honorable really does pay off in the end.

I have seen *Dirty Dancing* around 50 times! I know, but it is spread out over the 25 years, so it really isn't too bad. Myself, I love to dance, and watching them dance and seeing how cute Baby was when she was learning the dance reminded me of myself at times, but she had the hot partner. I wish there could have been a *Dirty Dancing* 2–100, all with Patrick, but that never happened. It has always left me wanting more. . . . I didn't want it to end. Thanks for continuing the memory of this great film.

CHAPTER THIRTEEN

FAN COMMENTS AT THE ANN ARBOR SUMMER FESTIVAL SCREENING OF *DIRTY DANCING*

On July 8, 2012, I randomly spoke to some of the fans prior to the outdoor screening of *Dirty Dancing* at the Ann Arbor Summer Festival in Ann Arbor, Michigan.

ELYSE AURBACH

What brought you to see *Dirty Dancing* tonight? I'm sure you've seen it before.

ELYSE: I have—yeah—about a million times. It's a good movie to watch in the summer—kind of everything.

And how about you, sir?

BOYFRIEND: This will be my second time seeing it and I'm seeing it because my girlfriend wants to see it.

How many times have you seen it?

ELYSE: I have no idea—a lot.

Over a hundred, you think?

ELYSE: Not over a hundred. Probably less than twenty, but I couldn't give you that exact number.

Okay. Do you have a favorite part of the movie? Favorite scene? Favorite actor/actress?

ELYSE: I like the scene where Baby and Johnny are dancing and then they get caught by what's-his-name—like, the creepy little guy.

Neil?

ELYSE: And, like, they're all sexy with each other and then they act all ashamed and then they get indignant. It's excellent.

Excellent. What do you think of them doing a remake of the movie?

ELYSE: What, the *Havana Nights*, or whatever it was?

No, Kenny Ortega is supposed to be the director of a remake.

ELYSE: A whole new remake?

Yeah, they put it on hold for now, but it was supposed to come out in 2013 and now they have it on hold until 2014.

ELYSE: Boo! Boo!

There's the one and only *Dirty Dancing*?

ELYSE: There's the one and only *Dirty Dancing*. There are some movies that were good the first time and just need to not be remade, because there's nothing that needs to be improved.

All right. Anything else you want to say about *Dirty Dancing*?

ELYSE: It's a great movie.

PATRICIA SPUDICH

What is it about *Dirty Dancing* that brings you here tonight?

PATRICIA: It always makes me feel happy after seeing it. Whenever I see it on TV, I always stop and watch it.

How many times have you seen it?

PATRICIA: I have no idea. I have seen pieces of it many, many times.

What do you think about making a remake of the movie?

PATRICIA: I don't know. It would be hard. I think the cast was a big part of why it was so good.

The main actors or the entire cast?

PATRICIA: The main ones and some of the supporting ones too. I can't imagine somebody else in those roles.

LISA AND ASHLEY

What brings you to see *Dirty Dancing* tonight?

LISA: This is my good friend, Ashley. We're here because, first of all, we love Patrick Swayze.

ASHLEY: She loves Patrick Swayze. I pretty much adore the movie, you know, and I adore true love, and "Nobody puts Baby in a corner," and good dancing, good music.

What do you think about them doing a remake of the movie?

ASHLEY: *Havana Nights*? It was okay. No, there actually is . . .

LISA: Another one.

Yes, Kenny Ortega is the director, but they've actually put it on hold until about 2014.

ASHLEY: I don't think it will be the same. It won't have the same vibe—I don't think. I don't think it will work. But I think any of us would be excited to see it.

LISA: Yeah, I would go see it because it would probably, you know, provide a new outlook—right? It would definitely be a newer vision of the story line. It could appeal to a younger crowd—like people that don't necessarily know those actors. I would be excited to see it.

ASHLEY: Yeah, I would watch it, but I would be a little skeptical watching it. . . . It's a classic. You know, how do you re-do that? I would watch it. I'd be excited to see it, but how do you do Patrick Swayze and Jennifer Grey? They made love something you didn't ever feel—that you always wanted to feel—so because of that, you just want to keep watching it over and over again. It's like a fantasy—right? It's a dream.

CHAPTER FOURTEEN

DIRTY DANCING MUSIC TRIVIA

1. The original soundtrack of *Dirty Dancing* was released in 1987—at the same time as the movie. It was #1 on the *Billboard* 200 album sales charts for 18 weeks and went multi-platinum.

2. The original edition had 12 songs: "(I've Had) The Time of My Life," "Be My Baby," "She's Like the Wind," "Hungry Eyes," "Stay," "Yes," "You Don't Own Me," "Hey Baby," "Overload," "Love Is Strange," "Where Are You Tonight?" and "In the Still of the Night."

3. By 2007, the *Dirty Dancing* soundtrack had sold more than 42 million copies. It continues to be one of the best-selling albums of all time.

4. In 1988, "*Dirty Dancing*: Live in Concert," the musical tour, featuring Bill Medley and Eric Carmen, went to 90 cities in 90 days. (I attended this fabulous show and I still have my souvenir button: "Things Go Better with *Dirty Dancing*.")

5. "(I've Had) The Time of My Life" was performed by Bill Medley and Jennifer Warnes. This performance was the first time they sang together.

6. "(I've Had) The Time of My Life" won an Oscar, Grammy, and Golden Globe in 1988.

7. "She's Like the Wind" was #3 on *Billboard* Hot 100 and #1 on *Billboard* Hot Adult Contemporary in 1989.

8. "She's Like the Wind" was originally written for (but never used in) the movie *Grandview, U.S.A.* (1984). The inspiration for the song was Lisa Niemi—Patrick Swayze's wife.

9. "She's Like the Wind" is only one of many songs written by Patrick Swayze. Other songs include: "Cliff's Edge" (used in *Road House*), "Brothers" (used in *Next of Kin*), "Finding My Way Back," and "When You Dance" (both used in *One Last Dance*).

10. In 1989, "She's Like the Wind" won at the BMI Film & TV Awards for most performed song from a film.

11. "Hungry Eyes," performed by Eric Carmen, was #4 on the *Billboard* Hot 100 charts in 1988 and #2 on *Billboard* Hot Adult Contemporary.

12. In 1960, Maurice Williams & the Zodiacs recorded Maurice's song "Stay." The song went to #1 on the national charts and remained there all summer.

13. In 1988, Maurice Williams was given a multi-platinum award for sales of more than 8 million copies of RCA Records soundtrack albums and cassettes.

14. In 1999, Maurice Williams was inducted into the South Carolina Music and Entertainment Hall of Fame and in 2004 received the Hennessy Privilege Award.

15. Sylvia Robinson and Mickey Baker recorded "Love Is Strange" in 1956.

16. "Love Is Strange" was inducted in to the GRAMMY Hall of Fame in 2004.

17. "Be My Baby" is a 1963 song written by Phil Spector, Jeff Barry, and Ellie Greenwich and performed by the Ronettes. It reached #2 on the US *Billboard* Pop Singles Chart and #4 on the UK's Record Retailer.

18. "Be My Baby" was inducted in to the GRAMMY Hall of Fame in 1999 and *Time* has the song on its list of the All-TIME 100 Songs.

19. Michael Lloyd was the producer for "Yes," "She's Like the Wind," and "(I've Had) The Time of My Life."

20. Reportedly, the television show *E! True Hollywood Story* episode of September 3, 2000 quoted Franke Previte as saying that before a single from the *Dirty Dancing* soundtrack had even been released, there were a million albums on back-order with RCA.

CHAPTER FIFTEEN

MORE ABOUT PATRICK SWAYZE'S PORTRAYAL OF JOHNNY CASTLE

Mitchell Krugel, author of the 1988 book *PATRICK SWAYZE*, quotes Pam Walker (who worked in the entertainment industry) commenting about Patrick Swayze's performance in *Dirty Dancing*:

> **"Swayze has a presence onscreen," she claimed. "When he walks into the room, all you want to do is take him home."[1]**

Irin Carmon, author of the article "*Dirty Dancing* Is The Greatest Movie Of All Time" (April 29, 2010, Jezebel.com) states:

> **And Johnny. *Johnny*. Nobody but Patrick Swayze could have done this, made Johnny so strong and yet so fragile. The new Keepsake DVD, released next week, has a tribute to him that, in addition to making me cry, points out that he was the son of a ballerina and a cowboy, a straight male dancer raised in a "redneck town" in Texas. No wonder his version of a masculine ideal was so generous and alluring.[2]**

Jay A. Fernandez from the *Hollywood Reporter* quotes Kenny Ortega in his article "Kenny Ortega to Direct 'Dirty Dancing' Remake" (August 8, 2011, Hollywoodreporter.com):

> **"Patrick Swayze set the bar for men dancing in the movies as Gene Kelly and Fred Astaire did before him."**[3]

Credit: Sue Tabashnik.

Patrick's Hollywood Walk of Fame star,
which he received on his 45th birthday on August 18, 1997.

CLOSING

Looking back on it, even though it was really hard to pull off and hard to shoot and we were choreographing it round the clock when we weren't shooting, and trying to turn a sweet little movie into something that really had something to say, we really did do a little magic here and I'm proud of it.

—Patrick Swayze speaking in 1997[1]

CANCER ORGANIZATIONS

THE PATRICK SWAYZE PANCREAS CANCER RESEARCH FUND

Stanford University
Development Services
PO Box 20466
Stanford, CA 94309
650-725-2504

http://cancer.stanford.edu/help/gift-PatrickSwayzeFund.html

"Gifts to this fund will support studies to increase our understanding of pancreas cancer and develop new therapies and technologies that can be applied to improving diagnosis, treatment, and prevention.

"'Our goal is to apply a multidisciplinary approach to the study of pancreas cancer and the care of patients afflicted with this disease,' says George A. Fisher, MD, PhD, associate professor medicine-oncology."

PANCREATIC CANCER ACTION NETWORK

1500 Rosencrans Avenue, Suite 200
Manhattan Beach, CA 90266
877-272-6226 or 310-725-0025

www.pancan.org

"The national organization creating hope in a comprehensive way through research, patient support, community outreach and advocacy for a cure."

STAND UP TO CANCER
File 1224
1801 W. Olympic Boulevard
Pasadena, CA 91199-1224
888-907-8263

www.standup2cancer.org

"This is where the end of cancer begins: when we unite in one unstoppable movement and Stand Up To Cancer."

AMERICAN CANCER SOCIETY
PO Box 22718
Oklahoma City, OK 73123-1718
800-227-2345

www.cancer.org

"We have spent more than $3.5 billion on cancer research since 1948 and have played a role in nearly every cancer breakthrough in recent history."

LEUKEMIA & LYMPHOMA SOCIETY
1311 Mamaroneck Avenue
Suite 310
White Plains, NY 10605
800-557-7177

www.lls.org

"The Leukemia & Lymphoma Society (LLS) is the world's largest voluntary health agency dedicated to blood cancer."

ACKNOWLEDGMENTS

When I started writing this book in March 2012, I had no idea that soon I would experience a very tough time in my life, including a near-death experience in May 2012 (which resulted in severe injuries) and the illness and then death of my dad from leukemia and cancer in January 2013. Many times the book became my savior. I am so grateful to all of the people who provided support, expertise, patience, and love to me.

I have special gratitude to Bob Howell, maverick myotherapist and dear friend, who passed away in January 2013. I miss you so much.

I thank my mentor, Lee Santiwan. I miss you so much. Yes, a second book!

I thank my family, especially my mom, Phyllis Friedman; my dad, David Tabashnik; my brothers, Bruce Tabashnik and David Tabashnik; my aunts, Nedra Kapetansky and Mary Lou Zieve; my step-mom Suzanne Tabashnik; my nephew Gabe Tabashnik; and Andrea Mathias. Also, thanks to my cousin Joanne Canvasser, who hung out with me in Ann Arbor to watch the outdoor screening of *Dirty Dancing* last summer, and my cousins Carol and Mike Golob for their support.

I thank my physicians, especially Dr. Y. Special gratitude to Dr. F for getting me through the past year. Special gratitude to Dr. O.

I thank police officers Craig Karinen and Rolando Rivera for saving my life.

I thank my friends—especially Mary Kiriazis, Don Frazier, Margaret Howden, Ingrid Mennella, Nancy Ruonavaara-Ingram,

Michelle Tukel, Cynthia Archer-Gift—and my many, many colleagues at work (you know who you are). A special shout-out to Quentin Calvert and assessment staff, Barb Bracye and registration staff, security staff, and ER staff.

I thank my amazing interviewees, who were all so gracious and generous: Linda Gottlieb, Maurice Williams, Jackie Horner, Rowena Adalid and the Madame Tussauds staff, Jim and Karen Myers, Tom and Patt Rocks, and Betty Rollins. A special thank-you to Joshua Sinclair for his moving tribute to Patrick Swayze and permission to use the official *Jump!* poster.

I thank the wonderful fans who wrote tributes and spoke to me about *Dirty Dancing*: Anna Mathias, Debbie Wallerstein, Elly Ali, Heidi Nielsen, Holly Tuell, Ingrid Mennella, Kelly Miner, Shirley Penrod, Tanya Holliday, Elyse Aurbach, Patricia Spudich, Lisa, and Ashley.

I could not have completed this book without the expert help and support of Patricia Bacall, book maverick and cover/book designer, and Nicole Klungle, editor extraordinaire. Your shepherding and expertise made all of the difference in the world.

I thank my expert attorney, Larry Jordan.

I thank the following people for supporting this project by putting me in touch with potential interviewees: Mike Porterfield, head chef at Mountain Lake Lodge; Harry Turner, president, Beach Music Association International; Laura Rowley, senior editor for the *Huffington Post*; Phil Dilanni, Rubenstein Communications, Inc.; Kim Kimzey, staff writer for the *Herald-Journal*; and David Henshall, writer for the *East Anglian Daily Times*.

I thank Buzz Scanland, consultant and former general manager at Mountain Lake Hotel (now known as Mountain Lake Lodge), for facilitating the use of photos. I thank Jamie Vuignier, manager of the Kobal Collection at Art Resource, for assistance with the *Dirty Dancing* stills. I thank Arabella Neville-Rolfe, publicist from Target Live, for the photos of the *Dirty Dancing* stage show performers. I thank DJ Rick Pruett for his photo of the Patrick Swayze memorial stone. I thank Murray Goldenberg for the author photo.

I thank Deana Dupree from St. Martin's Press for facilitating the use of quotes.

I thank John Gifford, amazing myotherapist.

I thank Laura Schuster, marvelous website designer.

I thank my family members and friends for inspiration I have derived from their courageous battles against cancer and pray for a time when cancer no longer exists.

Finally, I thank Linda Gottlieb, producer, for her Herculean work in creating/getting the movie made; Eleanor Bergstein, writer and co-producer, for creating the movie and fighting to have it made; and Emile Ardolino, Jennifer Grey, Patrick Swayze, Jerry Orbach, Cynthia Rhodes, Jack Weston, Jane Brucker, Kelly Bishop, Kenny Ortega, Miranda Garrison, and all of the people involved in making *Dirty Dancing*, as your creation is held so dear in the hearts of so many people!

ABOUT THE AUTHOR

Credit: Murray Goldenberg

Sue Tabashnik published her first book, *The Fans' Love Story: How the Movie* 'DIRTY DANCING' *Captured the Hearts of Millions!* in July 2010. She has been an active member of the Official Patrick Swayze International Fan Club since 2000 and has written numerous articles for the club magazine. During her thirty-six years as a master's level social worker, she has honed her interview skills while conducting thousands of interviews. She has brought her passion for and strong personal connection to *Dirty Dancing* with her social work background to write her unique *Dirty Dancing* tribute books. Sue has lived most of her life in the Detroit area.

Author website: www.likedirtydancing.com

A portion of the proceeds from the sale of this book will be donated to the Patrick Swayze Pancreas Cancer Research Fund at the Stanford Cancer Institute.